SEASONS OF YOUR HEART

SEASONS OF YOUR HEART

Prayers and Reflections

MACRINA WIEDERKEHR, O.S.B.

HarperSanFrancisco
A Division of HarperCollins*Publishers*

SEASONS OF YOUR HEART: *Prayers and Reflections, Revised and Expanded.*
Copyright © 1991 by Macrina Wiederkehr. All rights reserved. Printed
in the United States of America. No part of this book may be used or
reproduced in any manner whatsoever without written permission
except in the case of brief quotations embodied in critical articles and
reviews. For information address HarperCollinsPublishers, 10 East 53rd
Street, New York, NY 10022.

REVISED AND EXPANDED EDITION

(This revised and expanded edition is based on an edition published in
1979 by Silver Burdett Company.)

Library of Congress Cataloging-in-Publication Data

Wiederkehr, Macrina.
   Seasons of your heart : prayers and reflections / Macrina
Wiederkehr. — Rev. and expanded.
     p.   cm.
   Includes index.
   ISBN 0-06-069300-2
   1. Meditations. 2. Prayers. 3. Spiritual exercises. I. Title.
BX2182.2.W54 1991
242—dc20   90-55776
                                           CIP

97 98 99 RRD-H 20 19 18 17 16 15 14 13 12 11

To someone I recognized
in the breaking of bread:

John Bloms, O.S.B.

CONTENTS

Taking Off Your Shoes: The Season of Wonder   *1-30*

Like Moses I feel called to strip away the unnecessary in order to meet the wonder, so often hidden behind the clutter of my life. Sometimes when certain things are gone, the glory can be seen. It is the Season of Wonder. I am God's story of Wonder.

Standing on Tiptoe: The Season of Hope   *39-68*

Standing on tiptoe is not a children's game of balance. Rather, it is the beautiful prayer of balancing God's promises with my faith. It is the Season of Hope. I am God's story of Hope.

Washing Feet: The Season of Love   *75-106*

An old Quaker song tells me that when I have truly come to understand simplicity I will not be ashamed to bend and to bow. Washing feet requires a great deal of bending, resulting in a great deal of healing. It is the Season of Love. I am God's story of Love.

Racing to the Tomb: The Season of Mystery 113-148

With Peter and John I race to the tomb. I spend my days looking for life. The secret is: I must lose my life to find my life. I must die to live. It is the Season of Mystery. I am God's Mystery story.

Walking with Strangers: The Season of Faith 157-185

The power of the resurrection becomes visible as I come to trust the strangers I meet along the way. I begin to suspect who they are. I respond in faith to their needs. I live the gospel. It is the season of Faith. I am God's story of Faith.

Seasons of Your Heart would never have been published without the nudging of Chuck Bodmer and the encouragement of my first editor, Jack van Bemmel. Their assurance to me, a new writer, that my words had a message supported my own longing to write. My deepest gratitude goes to the readers, of my first edition of *Seasons of Your Heart.* Their many cards and letters continue to say in so many ways, "These seasons are our seasons. Your journey is our journey." Because of all this affirmation a new edition of *Seasons* has been born.

I give special thanks to my sisters in community who pray these seasons and walk this journey with me each day. From among my sisters I must single out three who have befriended the new manuscript for *Seasons* in special ways: Cabrini! Scholastica! Patricia! Thank you!

Finally, I am deeply grateful for two friends who have so often celebrated with me the seasons of my heart, Rachel Dietz, O.S.B. and Joyce Rupp, O.S.M. Over the years they have done much to energize my spirit and keep my writer's heart alive.

The journey theme has always held a special attraction for me. The first journey I can remember is my journey along the cow path on our farm in Arkansas. One of my childhood chores was to bring home the cows. To do this I had to walk through the woods to the pasture. These were my first meditation walks. As I walked the cow path, I would watch for little animals on the way. I would feast on the sight of all the wild flowers. Under some of the trees I would find layers and layers of green moss, which I imagined to be an outside carpet for the elves.

Wonder filled my young heart as I journeyed along the old cow path. Questions were born and mysteries solved. Indeed it became a walk filled with mystery. There were burning bushes everywhere I looked. All unknown to me at that fragile age I carried within my heart the seed of three virtues that were to be of untold value to me in my later years. Their names? Hope! Love! Faith! Along with Wonder and Mystery these have been significant seasons on my spiritual journey.

My feet have always taken me to places where my heart has whispered we should go. My heart has been a wonderful teacher. It is also my favorite burning bush. God keeps calling to me from the midst of it, getting my attention and directing my feet toward new paths. Some of these new paths have prompted me to revise and expand *Seasons of Your Heart*. I've grown up a lot since meandering along the old cow paths. I've even done a little growing since the first edition of this book was published. A revised, expanded edition of a book gives the book a chance to grow up with its author.

Some of my new journeys have acquainted me with prophets whose cries have changed my life. My heart has been newly awakened to many injustices throughout the world that we have lived with far too long.

My retreat ministry has led me to the holy ground of much brokenness and woundedness in people's lives. At the same time I have become truly aware of the tremendous potential for healing in the human spirit. The unfailing power of prayer and the connectedness of those who pray with and for one another have renewed my hope.

These reflections and prayers, then, have grown out of a daily listening to God in the changing seasons of my spiritual life. My seasons keep changing. My heart keeps burning. My feet keep moving.

The seasons of my heart change like the seasons of the fields. There are seasons of wonder and hope, seasons of suffering and love, seasons of healing. There are seasons of dying and rising, seasons of faith.

I am part of the earth that God wants to share with the world. I am God's story told in the changing colors of autumn, winter, spring, and summer. When I pray, my heart cries out the story of my life. These prayers have been born out of my seasonal struggle with God. I share with you the seasons of my heart. Perhaps, in some way, they are the seasons of your heart. This book is meant to be a companion, a kind of prayer book, to bless you as you walk with God through the seasons of your heart.

These reflections have grown out of my conviction that our God is not some Almighty Being beyond us, but a Mystery within. There is a part of us that cannot rest until it knows completion. We suspect, on days when our eyes are wide open, that most things in life are passing. We watch life come and go. Our hearts change with the seasons. But deep inside, where it's hard to reach, most of us believe there is something about us that will outlast those changing seasons—something that will never die. We spend much of our lives trying to understand this Mystery within.

Perhaps you have also felt within you this stirring of the eternal. Praying with this book, then, will be a little like a journey into yourself, a walk through the seasons of your heart. It will, of course, be a journey unfinished, for our call into the depths of who we are is so vast that no one can show us how to get there in a lifetime, and surely not in one small book.

The God we walk with has many faces. We call these faces shown to us, Revelation. We call the walk with God, Communion. You are invited to walk slowly. Watch for the change of seasons as you walk, and notice how bits of other seasons linger in every walk.

The Journey

As you prayerfully walk through these pages there will be images along the way to help you with your journey. Each symbol suggests a mental posture for you to adopt. Each suggests a way of tapping the eternal within you.

"Taking Off Your Shoes" is a call to let go. It's a call to emptiness and poverty, to detachment and simplicity. It holds out to you the *wonder* that's possible when the clutter is gone. This is truly the season of *wonder*.

"Standing on Tiptoe" calls you to vision, expectation, and birth. It is the Epiphany season, inviting you to see what is difficult to see. It is the season of *hope*.

"Washing Feet" is a call to service, to conversion. It is the season of your birth as a disciple. It says, "No," to any form of apathy. It is the season of *love*.

"Racing to the Tomb" asks of you the willingness to die and rise. This season encourages you to risk walking through the known into the unknown. It calls you to journey through the Paschal Mystery. Indeed, it is the season of *mystery*.

"Walking with Strangers" is a call to ministry and to belief in the power of the resurrection in your daily life. This is the season that asks you to put away your fear and live these words of St. Teresa of Avila: "Christ has no body now on earth but yours." This is the season of *faith*.

As you consider the image of taking off your shoes (or any of the other images), hold it up against the eternal in you. Connections can be made that make growth and healing possible. It takes practice and discipline. It requires a great deal of listening and stillness, but it can happen. The more often this growth and healing begins to take place in your life, the greater will be the possibility for a rich and deep prayer life.

The scripture passages, reflections, and poems contained here are not only meant to be read but are also intended for reflective listening. Merely reading them would be like running through a friend's house, in the front door and out the back, without stopping for a visit. It is difficult to tap the eternal by just hastily passing through.

This is an invitation to a journey within. There's a road that runs straight through your heart. Walk along that road and you may at any moment stumble upon the Mystery that there is no other name for, save God.

A Guide for Your Journey

The following suggestions have been prepared to discourage you from rushing through your prayer. You are encouraged, instead, to linger with each scripture passage as you would linger with a friend. If you use these suggestions you may more easily stumble upon the mystery that so often remains hidden because you hurry.

Choose a place to pray where you can be comfortable. Let it be a familiar place where you can take off your shoes and be at home with yourself.

You may want to use a simple decoration as a symbol of the scripture passage with which you are praying. Some possibilities include: a flower, a bowl of water, a rock, a plant, a stem of wheat, an earthen vessel, a candle, some fruit, a piece of bread and/or a glass of wine, a sunrise or sunset, a tree, a pair of shoes, a road, a window, a teddy bear, a picture of a friend, a cross, a lump of clay, an empty cup, a crumbled leaf, a jar of perfume.

As you begin your journey, keep in mind that this is a journey unfinished. You can always go deeper into the mystery of who you are. You can always stop for a visit instead of hastily passing through.

This guide for your meditation is only a suggestion. It is not meant to glue you into a mold or to be the only route you can follow. When you go on a trip you use a road map to verify a number of things before deciding which route to take. There is seldom only one way to go. Depending on how much time you have, and what kind of mood you are in, you may want to take a scenic route. If your time is limited, you may choose the most direct route. If you are going to do some errands along the way, you might have to go down a few side roads. The important thing to remember is that a map is only a guide; it presents options if you are free enough and flexible enough to use them. This guide for your journey is similar to a map; use it if you find it helpful.

· Read the scripture passage carefully.
· Sit quietly and discern its meaning for you.
· Strive to put yourself into the reading:
  Become the person read about.
  Imagine that you are the bread, broken and shared.
  Experience the poverty of the one who needs healing.
  Be the person who is healed. *Be* the healer.
  Identify with the struggle and blessing of the passage.

Linger with the images that come to you.

Allow these images to ask you questions about your life.

- Read the scripture passage a second time, aloud if possible.
- How can these words become flesh in your life?
- Now read the reflection following the scripture.
- Savor it. Listen to it with the ear of your heart.
- Find some way to celebrate its message.

A Word about Celebration

Celebration is not entertainment. It is deeper. It grows out of a strong conviction, a passion, that needs your response. The finest way I know to celebrate is to be radically present to the message received. You do not have to be loud to celebrate, but you do need to be present with quality. Here are some suggestions to help you celebrate the God who visits you during your prayer.

- Attend to the message of your meditation throughout the day. Take it to your work. Take it to your play.
- Over a cup of tea share your meditation with a friend.
- Use a quote from the passage with which you prayed and make a greeting card for someone.
- Design a banner or a poster for your room.
- Write your own reflection or poem in your journal.
- Take a slow, reflective walk tasting the scripture that you prayed along the way.
- Choose a symbol that flows from your prayer. Place the symbol where you will see it often during the day as a reminder to celebrate the God who came to you during your prayer.

The Prayer Section

The prayers at the end of each chapter can serve as one last link with that chapter's theme. For example, when you finish praying chapter one, move into the section entitled "Prayers for Taking Off Your Shoes." These prayers are meant to encourage you to linger a few more days to celebrate the spirit of that season. You may also want to use this space to write some prayers of your own.

This is another attempt to slow you down, to keep you in the holy ground of one particular season for a while before sending you off on a new journey. Then, when your heart tells you it is time to move on, walk slowly into the next chapter.

The SEASON of WONDER

When I was a child wading in the brook I understood totally the needlessness of shoes. Shoes in a brook are only for the overcautious, for those who would not dare to risk a stubbed toe. But there is no way to go through life without stubbed toes. At least, there is no beautiful way—no holy way.

There will come a time in your life when the only sacred thing left to do is to take off your shoes. Take off your shoes to celebrate:

- the holy ground of your life
- the rushing waters of a brook
- the good earth or
- God speaking to you from a burning bush.

There are things in your life that prevent you from experiencing the Season of Wonder. Getting rid of these things can be like a call to take off your shoes. The meditations in this section ask you to

- take off your shoes
- investigate burning bushes
- give up false gods
- peel off layers of ego
- take down walls of separation
- strip away the unnecessary
- wait with patience
- say good-bye so the Spirit can come
- remove all obstacles to *wonder*
- walk barefoot in creek beds delighted and unafraid.

If you should ever hear God speaking to you from a burning bush, and it happens more often than most of us realize, *take off your shoes* for the ground on which you stand is holy.

The Birth of a Prophet

Moses was looking after the flock of Jethro, his father-in-law, priest of Midian. He led the flock to the far side of the wilderness and came to Horeb, the mountain of God. There the angel of Yahweh appeared to him in the shape of a flame of fire, coming from the middle of a bush. Moses looked; there was the bush blazing but it was not being burnt up. "I must go and look at this strange sight," Moses said, "and see why the bush is not burned." Now Yahweh saw him go forward to look, and God called to him from the middle of the bush. "Moses, Moses!" he said. "Here I am," he answered. "Come no nearer," he said. "Take off your shoes, for the place on which you stand is holy ground."

(Exodus 3:1–5, JB)

Only when Moses gave his attention to this fiery sign did God speak to him out of those flames. What does this say about the burning bushes of our own lives? What are the signs that, perhaps, we must turn aside to see if we are to hear God's voice today?

And the shoes? They too have a message. We struggle so to be holy. We yearn for the divine. Yet, how often we are standing on holy ground and need only take off our shoes to strip away whatever prevents us from experiencing the holy. I believe that God speaks to us in the burning bushes of today, and the message is still one of a holy ground that we miss because of unnecessary shoes.

So remember. If God ever speaks to you out of the flames *take off your shoes* and allow the prophet within you to be born.

> The Moses in my heart trembles
> not quite willing
> to accept the prophet hidden in my being
> wondering how much it will cost
> to allow that prophet to emerge.
>
> O child of unnecessary shoes
> cast them off
> and stand in readiness
> on this holy ground.
> For the Egypt in people's lives
> demands that you see the burning bushes
> all around you
> aflame
> burning wildly
> calling you
> away from the comfort
> of well-protected feet.
>
> The ground you stand on is holy.
> Take off your shoes!
> The ground of your being is holy.
> Take off your shoes!
> Awaken your sleeping prophet
> Believe in your Moses
> and go. . .

Child of Wonder

Praise Yahweh, my soul
I will praise Yahweh all my life,
I will make music to my God as long as I live.

(Psalm 146:1)

To be this child of wonder you must learn to take off your shoes often. Taking off your shoes is a sacred ritual. It is a hallowed moment of remembering the goodness of space and time. It is a way of celebrating the *holy ground* on which you stand. If you want to be a child of wonder cherish the truth that time and space are holy. Whether you take off your shoes symbolically or literally matters little. What is important is that you are alive to the *holy ground* on which you stand and to the *holy ground* that you are.

My bare feet walk the earth reverently
for everything keeps crying,
Take off your shoes
The ground you stand on is holy
The ground of your being is holy.

When the wind sings through the pines
  like a breath of God
  awakening you to the sacred present
  calling your soul to new insights
Take off your shoes!

When the sun rises above your rooftop
  coloring your world with dawn
  Be receptive to this awesome beauty

Put on your garment of adoration
Take off your shoes!

When the Red Maple drops its last leaf of summer
  wearing its "burning bush" robes no longer
  read between its barren branches, and
Take off your shoes!

When sorrow presses close to your heart
  begging you to put your trust in God alone
  filling you with a quiet knowing
  that God's hand is not too short to heal you
Take off your shoes!

When a new person comes into your life
  like a mystery about to unfold
  and you find yourself marveling over
  the frailty and splendor of every human being
Take off your shoes!

When, during the wee hours of the night
  you drive slowly into the new day
  and the morning's fog, like angel wings
  hovers mysteriously above you
Take off your shoes!

Take off your shoes of distraction
Take off your shoes of ignorance and blindness
Take off your shoes of hurry and worry
Take off anything that prevents you
from being *a child of wonder.*

Take off your shoes;
The ground you stand on is holy.
The ground you are is holy.

The Sacrament of Letting Go

That is why I am telling you not to worry about
your life and what you are to eat, nor about your
body and what you are to wear. Surely life is more
than food, and the body more than clothing! Look at
the birds in the sky. They do not sow or reap or
gather into barns; yet your heavenly Father feeds
them. Are you not worth much more than they are?

(Matthew 6:25–26)

I worry too much. Autumn trees ask me not to worry.
They, like Jesus, suggest trust rather than worry. So often in
autumn I want to go lean my head against a tree and ask
what it feels like to lose so much, to be so empty, so de-
tached, to take off one's shoes that well, and then simply to
stand and wait for God's refilling. It sounds so simple, so
easy. It isn't easy. But it's possible.

I think I've met one person in my lifetime who was truly
empty. I didn't ask her what it felt like, but I remember a
quiet joy that seemed to permeate her spirit, and she looked
free.

We autumn strugglers must try hard not to wear discouragement as a cloak if we can't wear enough emptiness
to make us free. It takes a long time to get as far as even
wanting to be empty.

Our hearts are hungering for the *Sacrament of Letting Go*.
Once we discover that we already possess enough grace to
let go, trust begins to form in the center of who we are.
Then we can take off our shoes and stand empty and vulnerable, eager to receive God's next gift.

And let us pray for one another, for emptying is painful, and the Body of Christ who we are calls us to support each other in this autumn effort. The Body of Christ also stands stripped, crucified, waiting for the new life that each of us can bring to it.

> Slowly
> she celebrated the sacrament of *letting go*
> first she surrendered her *green*
> then the *orange, yellow,* and *red*
> finally she let go of her *brown*
> shedding her last leaf
> she stood empty and silent, stripped bare.
> Leaning against the winter sky
> she began her vigil of trust.

> And Jesus said:

Why do you worry about clothes? Remember the flowers growing in the fields; they do not fret about what to wear; yet I assure you not even Solomon in all his royal robes was dressed like one of these.

> Shedding her last leaf
> she watched its journey to the ground.
> She stood in silence
> wearing the color of emptiness,
> her branches wondering:
> How do you give shade with so much gone?

> And Jesus said:

Do not be troubled or needlessly concerned.

> And then,
> the sacrament of waiting began.
> The sunrise and sunset watched with tenderness.
> Clothing her with silhouettes
> they kept her hope alive.

They helped her understand that
her vulnerability
her dependence and need
her emptiness
her readiness to receive
were giving her a new kind of beauty.
Every morning and every evening
they stood in silence
and celebrated together
the sacrament of waiting!

And Jesus said:

Now if that is how God cares for the wild flowers
in the fields which are here today and gone tomorrow, will He not all the more care for you. . .?

Understanding Your Wounds

I do not understand my own behavior; I do not act
as I mean to, but I do things that I hate.

(Romans 7:15)

Paul's cry of anguish has a universal ring to it. Who of us
has not felt deeply the frustration of being trapped in ad-
dictive behaviors from which we would like to be delivered?
Those behaviors that have become deep wounds in our spir-
its? Those that keep our true selves in bondage?

In praying about my wounds I have come to believe that
the reason these wounds take so long to heal is that I spend
more time attacking them than trying to understand them.
I keep trying to clog up the hole made by the wound. The
reality is that I keep stuffing my wound with other addictions, always hoping for some miraculous cure. The healing
needs to happen right there in that broken place because it is

there that I am vulnerable. It is there in that crack in my spirit that the Light of Christ can slip through and help me understand the wound. When Jesus rose, his wounds were still visible. The scars could be seen right in the midst of the glory. Is my life, patterned after Christ, to be any different?

The scars in my life have become my badges of victory and glory. Some healing has taken place, yet as I pray with these scars I am able to see that I will probably have to live with some of the pain I've inherited from my cluttered life. I am learning to befriend the scars and find the gifts hidden underneath.

Sometimes the scars open up again and I see that the wounds are not completely healed. I approach my wounds differently now though. The clutter that I once used to clog up these wounds, I now send away. I send it on its way gently. It has been a tool that God used to help me experience my powerlessness. In some mysterious way, then, my clutter becomes my treasure.

Slowly, gently
I lift the clutter out of my life
I must let go of my ego-self.
I've known this part of myself intimately.
It's like an old friend.
It's a bit hard to send it on its way.
It has become a kind of cherished sin for me
    a dis-ease that I am familiar with.
Still, it has ' ˦dered my growth
    and kept   from adoring.
It has prevented me from noticing
    the *holy ground* of my life.

And so, I kiss it good-bye.
Yes, I kiss it.
I embrace it.
It is part of myself

I cannot simply cast it aside.
I pray for its conversion.
All the clutter in my life
  that I have clung to
  with such devotion
  will be born again
  in some new and better form.

It is the shadow side of myself.
If I befriend it
  it will arise
  from the ashes of falseness
  into the glory of truth.

My uncontrollable anger
  becomes a passionate, prophetic zeal.
My possessive clutching
  becomes a generous giving.
My abundance of unnecessary words
  melts into the one *great word*.
My deafening noise
  becomes the sound of silence.
My need for approval from others
  becomes a need to affirm others.
My need to control
  becomes my need to share.
My fear is changed into love
  my anxiety into trust.

Yes, all the clutter of my life
  that ego stuff that held me back
  when embraced and owned
  can change before my very eyes into grace.
What was a hindrance becomes a blessing.
What was an enemy becomes a friend.
What was darkness is now my light.
What was my clutter is now my treasure.

There is no freedom
  like seeing myself as I am
  and not losing heart.
There is no freedom
  like looking at myself as I am
  and saying, "Yes, that's me!"
There is no freedom
  like taking myself in my arms.
Only in that embrace
  will I understand my wounds.
Only in that embrace
  will I experience healing.
Only in that embrace
  will I come to know my true self.

The Prize

Not that I have become perfect yet: I have not yet
won, but I am still running, trying to capture the
prize for which Christ Jesus captured me. I can assure you . . . I am far from thinking that I have already won. All I can say is that I forget the past and
I strain ahead for what is still to come; I am racing
for the finish, for the prize to which God calls us
upward to receive in Christ Jesus.

(Philippians 3:12–14, JB)

Defenses are unnecessary walls that we use when we seek to
protect the truth we are afraid isn't in us. These walls become the very obstacles that keep us separated from the
prize we are striving to attain. The prize is our true self
hidden with Christ in God. On our Christian journey we are

asked to let these defenses go. We are called to run forward and claim the truth that we have been grasped by Christ. We are a flame of Christ-life. Lived out, all this can mean for the folks whose lives we touch is *blessing*. We are a people who bear Christ's name. To deserve that name, our lives must bless. And so the barriers of our defenses will need to be surrendered. We must let them go. Only then can we claim the prize: life on high in Christ Jesus.

> when i let
> my defenses go
> *blessings* came running
>
> and there appeared stars
> i had never seen before
>
> shining
>   to me
>   for me
>
> and then suddenly
>   in me
>   and through me
>
> i ran forward
> carrying the torch
> bearing the prize
> God-possessed
> a star shining
>
> when i let my defenses go.

A Look of Love

. . . Jesus looked at him with love and told him, "There is one thing more you must do. Go and sell what you have and give to the poor; you will then

13

have treasure in heaven. After that, come and follow me." At these words the man's face fell. He went away sad, for he had many possessions.

(Mark 10:21–22, NA)

I always find this Gospel of Mark haunting. Jesus' look of love pursues me wherever I go. I am the rich young man walking away sad. I've done everything except give everything. The gift of total surrender is close at hand, still I fail to let it make its home in me. Yet even as I walk away, this nameless man's story echoes in my soul: . . .*and Jesus looked on him with love.* Like an unfinished song it haunts me: *and Jesus looks on me with love.* And though I walk away sad, Jesus' look of love follows me.

> The rich young man
>   inside of me
>   is sad.
> I, too, am about to go away.
>
> I am the one being called today.
> I am asked to empty myself
>   to strip my life of the unnecessary
>   to evaluate my possessions
>   to leave everything and follow
> Christ.
>
> Long have I heard this call.
> Deep within, it is being carved.
> It cuts into the very core of me.
> It doesn't allow me to forget.
>
> I wear it like a wound
>   that needs healing,
> rather than a call
>   that needs obedience.

Only one thing is necessary:
Leave all.

I turn to the rich young man of history
    and ask for grace.

I, too, am about to go away
    followed always
    by that look of love.

Baptized with Truth

Yahweh sent the prophet Nathan to David. He came
to him and said: "In the same town were two men,
one rich, the other poor. The rich man had flocks
and herds in great abundance; the poor man had
nothing but a ewe lamb, only a single little one
which he had bought. He fostered it and it grew up
with him and his children, eating his bread, drinking
from his cup, sleeping in his arms; it was like a
daughter to him. When a traveler came to stay, the
rich man would not take anything from his own
flock or herd to provide for the wayfarer who had
come to him. Instead he stole the poor man's lamb
and prepared that for his guest."

David flew into a great rage with the man. "As
Yahweh lives," he said to Nathan, "the man who
did this deserves to die. For doing such a thing and
for having shown no pity, he shall make fourfold
restitution for the lamb."

Nathan then said to David, "You are the man!"

(2 Samuel 12:1–7)

If scripture is to become my teacher, I must put on each
story like a robe to be worn, identifying with the characters,
walking in their shoes, feeling with their hearts.

This lovely passage from the Old Testament has worn well in my soul, empowering me to look at the lies of my life. I am a David-figure longing for a prophet like Nathan to baptize me with the truth.

I carry the prophet Nathan
  in my heart.
I am challenged to the bone
  as David was challenged,
That man is you!
I hear it in the center
  of everything that feels in me.

I am the one
  who proclaims another's death sentence
  only to discover,
  the sentence is mine.
I have slaughtered other's lambs
  and saved my own.

Only one thing is necessary:
  conversion
  a change of heart.

I turn to Nathan
  and am baptized with truth.

That man is you!

Bleeding and Believing

Now there was a woman suffering from a hemorrhage for the past twelve years, whom no one had been able to cure. She came up behind him and touched the fringe of his cloak; and the hemorrhage stopped at that very moment. Jesus said, "Who was it that touched me?" When they all denied it, Peter said, "Master, it is the crowds round you, pushing." But Jesus said, "Somebody touched me. I felt that power had gone out from me." Seeing herself discovered, the woman came forward trembling, and falling at his feet explained in front of all the people why she had touched him and how she had been cured at that very moment. "My daughter," He said, "your faith has saved you; go in peace."

(Luke 8:43–48)

That woman is you! I don't know what your hemorrhage looks like, but I have little doubt that something in you is bleeding. I don't know what your faith looks like, but I have little doubt that something in you is believing. And so really, that's enough. All you need do is to approach Jesus, bleeding and believing. The hem will be enough for touching. Power, like that, moving through you will help you understand your wound. Once you understand a wound it loses its power to destroy you. I know. That woman is me! I've been to the hem of God's garment. Let me tell you my story.

> Once there was a wound
> It was no ordinary wound
> It was *my* wound
> We had lived together long.
>
> I yearned to be free of this wound
> I wanted the bleeding to stop
> Yet if the truth be known
> I felt a strange kind of gratitude
>   for this wound

It had made me
   tremendously open to grace
   vulnerable to God's mercy.

A beautiful believing in me
   that I have named Faith
   kept growing, daring me
   to reach for what I could not see.
This wound had made me open.
I was ready for grace
And so one day, I reached.

There I was thick in the crowd
   bleeding and believing
   and I reached.
At first I reached
   for what I *could* see
   the fringe of a garment,
But my reaching didn't stop there
   for Someone reached back into
   me.
A grace I couldn't see
   flowed through me.
A power I didn't understand
   began to fill the depths of me.

Trembling I was called forth
   to claim my wholeness.
The bleeding had left me.
The believing remained
And strange as this may sound
I have never lost my gratitude
   for the wound
   that made me so open
   to grace.

Decorations

Now be patient . . . until the Lord's coming. Think
of a farmer: how patiently he waits for the precious
fruit of the ground until it has had the autumn rains
and the spring rains! You too must be patient; do
not lose heart, because the Lord's coming will be
soon.   *(James 5:7–8)*

In our search for the holy, there are times when our restless
preparations smother the very truth for which we are
searching. We decorate our rooms and make elaborate preparations for our prayer, when a single flower and a moment
of waiting are all we need to meet the One Who Comes. In
our restlessness, our search sometimes becomes the only
god we ever meet.

My days are all spent
in decorating my house.
I am forever preparing
for your arrival.
I hunger for your presence
yet I take not the time
to wait for your coming
and to my great sorrow
you never arrive.

It is because I refuse
to be silent
that I cannot hear you.

It is because I refuse
to await you
that you cannot come.

It is because I refuse
to be idle
that I cannot enjoy you.

It is because I am too busy
hanging decorations
that I cannot welcome you home.

Yet in your deep wisdom
your presence leans toward mine.
You understand my decorations
to be symbols of my hunger
and you know of the day
when my heart swept clean
will be the only decoration needed
and I will listen for your coming
like night awaiting day.

On the Morality of Holding on to Teddy Bears

People were bringing little children to him, for him
to touch them. The disciples scolded them, but when
Jesus saw this he was indignant and said to them,
"Let the little children come to me; do not stop
them; for it is to such as these that the kingdom of
God belongs. In truth I tell you, anyone who does
not welcome the kingdom of God like a little child
will never enter it." Then he embraced them, laid his
hands on them and gave them his blessing.

(Mark 10:13–16)

There is a *child* in us who must stay alive if we are to grow in holiness. It is the same child Jesus placed in our midst when he told us that we could hardly expect to handle heaven unless we become like that child. The tired adult in us often needs to be reminded that we are in charge of that child. You and I have the power to let it live or to bring about its early death. And so, my much-too-adult heart challenges you today: Go set free someone else's child by believing in your own. Take off your shoes and go. It's much like leading folks out of Egypt. Believe in your Moses and go. . .

Once upon a time
when days were still fresh
and new,
ordinary
and uncomplicated,
I was a free child
in love with everything. . .

a bee buzzing
the wind in my hair
a branch to hang from
bare feet in the grass
dandelions and fairies
teddy bears.

I don't remember growing up.
It must have happened while I wasn't looking
but it is obvious from my heart
that it has happened
for I am less simple
more complicated
and more cluttered.

I would not choose
to become a child again
but I am looking to children
and searching in them
for a simplicity and ordinariness
that makes being an adult
easier to accept
and miracles easier to see.

Children are not too sophisticated
to wonder
to take off their shoes
to reach out, and up
and all around
for that's where miracles are.

The child in me longs
to touch all of the adults I know
with the magic wand of littleness
and perform that great miracle
of enabling them to understand
that it's not too late
to live happily ever after.
The problem is so simple
they could miss it.
Their teddy bears
they've thrown too far
and how desperately they need them.

Jesus Is or Is Not Lord

Make your own the mind of Christ Jesus: Who, being in the form of God did not count equality with
God something to be grasped. But he emptied himself, taking the form of a slave, becoming as human
beings are; and being in every way like a human be-

ing, He was humbler yet, even to accepting death,
death on a cross. And for this God raised him high,
and gave him the name which is above all other
names; so that all beings in the heavens, on earth
and in the underworld, should bend the knee at the
name of Jesus and that every tongue should acknowledge Jesus Christ as Lord, to the glory of God
the Father.   *(Philippians 2:5–11)*

We search for a God we can touch. In our longing for such
a God we often create false gods who seem not so demanding. It is hard for us to admit the truth that what we worship
and serve really is Lord of our lives. Jesus *is* or *is not* Lord!
As we come to understand our Christian call, we are able to
see more clearly that the middle road makes little sense and
is often nothing more than apathy. Either Jesus is Lord of
our lives or he is not. The middle road is, perhaps, the most
dangerous road of all.

I woke up one day and realized I was on that most dangerous road. It wasn't holy ground. It was middle ground.
Safe ground! I wanted to get close to the fire without being
burned. I created my gods carefully and carried them in the
processions of my life, making sure they wouldn't scar me
in any way. But the fire burned out of control, my control
that is, and I was burned. That scar turned out to be the
most beautiful scar of my life.

> The God I was trying to love
> was too demanding
> And so I looked for other gods
> who would ask less of me
> And in unconverted corners of my heart
> I found them
> waiting to be adored
> asking nothing of me

yet making me a slave.
Possessions, recognition, power!
I bowed before them but my hunger
only deepened.

The God I was trying to escape
was too loving
so He sent me a brother, Jesus
to be my Lord
and to free me from my false gods
But this Lord Jesus
preached a hard gospel
and so I turned to other lords
and Jesus was not my Lord
   —except on Sundays for a little while
     because it is the custom
     for those who wish to bear the name
     Christian
     to gather for worship
     on that day—
But Jesus was not my Lord
And my idol-filled life
was a banner that proclaimed:
Jesus is not Lord!

The God I was trying to love
was too loving
and too demanding
so He gathered up my false gods
  my reputation, my pride
  my honor and prestige
  my possessions, my success
  my own glory
  my time
  even my friends.
He gathered up all these lords of mine.

He gathered up all my lies
and held them close to me
so close, I lost all sight
of my true God for a while.

But my true God never lost sight of me
And in that lies my salvation
for in one desperate moment
smothered by gods who couldn't save me
I prayed for a God who would
fill my lies with truth.
I prayed for a God who would
expect something of me,
a God who would be too loving
and too demanding
to be patient with my false gods any longer.

God heard that prayer
and loved me
I was given back to myself,
and taught
how to answer my own prayer
so that with other believers
I might again proclaim:

Jesus Christ is Lord!

Roots and Wings

. . . I live now not with my own life but with the
life of Christ who lives in me.

(Galatians 2:20, JB)

Good-byes have been some of the most difficult moments
of my life until Paul blessed me with his vision in Gala-

tians 2:20. "And I live now not with my own life but with the life of Christ who lives in me." I wind in and out of people's lives. Having touched them, I am blessed. Having touched me, they are blessed. Our roots are deepened. Our wings are strengthened. We have given each other grace to live more deeply. We have, indeed, become a part of one another in the Body of Christ. It is the incarnation taking place again. And then the war begins, that beautiful war between my roots and my wings. It feels as though my feet are in two worlds. It hurts. I look at all the people I love. I know the day will come when I must celebrate good-bye with them as I already have with so many others.

And yet, I am grafted into the Body of Christ. I never knew it could be so intimate until I was startled by a new vision: I live now, not I, but Bernice, Larry, Joyce, Nicholas, Timothy, live on in me. You will always be a part of me, for you were present during so much of my unfolding. My good-bye to you says that you've given me enough roots to use my wings. Still, it remains a struggle, this war between my roots and wings.

Roots and wings
I yearn for most of all
My longing to stay
My longing to go, come
wrapped in the same package.
I struggle.

It is very much the same
when we fall into each other's lives.
Our roots say:
  Stay!
    Set up your tent!
    Be at home here!

Our wings say:
    Continue your journey!
    Don't get root bound!
    Keep dreaming of something beyond!

When you love someone
you have to let them go.
It's the only way to keep them.

Weaving in and out of lives
I've come to know
the letting go
as the surrender in that war
between my roots and wings.
It is blessing!
It is grace!
It is victory!
It is pain!

Paul felt it too (Philippians 1:21–26)
anguishing over
his place on earth
his home in heaven.

I live now
not I
but you,
all of you,
live on in me.

I never knew the Body of Christ could be so intimate.

Ascension

. . .you will receive the power of the Holy Spirit
which will come on you, and then you will be my

witnesses not only in Jerusalem but throughout Judea and Samaria, and indeed to earth's remotest end.

As he said this he was lifted up while they looked on, and a cloud took him from their sight. They were still staring into the sky as he went when suddenly two men in white were standing beside them and they said, "Why are you Galileans standing here looking into the sky? This Jesus who has been taken up from you into heaven will come back in the same way as you have seen Him go to heaven."

(Acts of the Apostles 1:8–11)

I have always looked upon the Feast of the Ascension as a tremendous act of faith in us. Jesus, in leaving us, tells us that we are ready to be the Body of Christ, the Church on earth. Even stronger than his physical departure is the proclamation that if he does not go away, the Spirit cannot come (John 16:7). When I try to pray and live the Ascension, two images come to my mind: autumn trees and departing friends.

Once, on an autumn day very near the edge of winter, I stood like the friends of Jesus, gazing upward toward an almost empty tree. The leaves seemed to be saying to the tree: Unless we go away, you cannot be renewed. We have to die. We must return to the earth. We have to let go of you so you can be reborn.

And how often, in airports, I've stood gazing upward toward ascending planes remembering Jesus' words: "Unless I go away, the Spirit cannot come." Sometimes we have to be left on our own to discover the uniqueness and strength that is ours. It is as though in leaving, whether it be of Jesus, a friend, or a leaf, something of them returns to convince us that we are not alone. We have not been abandoned. We have, perhaps, in that leaving been given the gift of ourselves in a new, deeper, and more lasting way.

Ascensions into heaven are like falling leaves
sad and happy all at the same time
Going away isn't really sad
especially when your going
enables a new kind of presence
to be born.

Long have the leaves known the trees
They've danced together
in the wind
days upon days.
But now, growing older
and wiser,
they know they can't cling
to the trees forever.
And so they say good-bye
falling to the ground
waiting for the mystery of death
to transform them
into nourishment for the earth.

And the trees?
They stand alone for one short season
but they are at peace,
waiting for another mystery
to enfold them
with its presence.

When I saw you leaving
    I covered my face with my heart
    Oh, the ache of letting go
    But then I remembered the trees
    and so I stood in peace
    remembering your return.

When you come back
  we will be new for each other.
  Much will have happened in our lives.
  There will be more for each of us to love
  more for each of us to know.
  The Spirit will have left a footprint
  in our lives,
  and we will be excited
  like a new leaf
    come home
      to a tree!

Prayer for Taking Off Your Shoes

Creator of fire and water,
Your burning bush has turned
  into a bubbling brook
And I have taken off my shoes
  having heard you call my name.

You do not speak in fire only, Lord.
In water you have sung your songs
And you are singing still.
Today you chant a memory-song
  to my grown-up heart.

You are washing my anxiety away
You are reminding me of days of old
  when I had time to play.
I stand barefoot upon the stones
  the rushing water,
  lapping at my heels.
The sharp stones pierce my grown-up soles
My tough child-feet have worn away
  as I grew up, forgetting to play.

Creator of the rocks and streams,
I'm growing up once more
I'm taking off my shoes
  and remembering to adore.

My feet are getting tough again
My heart is getting young.

The Prayer of the Empty Water Jar

Jesus, I come into the warmth of your presence
   knowing that you are
   the very emptiness of God.
I come before you
   holding the water jar of my life.
Your eyes meet mine
   and I know what I'd rather not know.

I came to be filled
   but I am already full.
I am too full
This is my sickness
I am full of things
   that crowd out
   your healing presence.
A holy knowing steals inside my heart
   and I see the painful truth.
I don't need more
I need less
I am too full.

I am full of things that block out
   your golden grace.
I am smothered by gods of my own creation
I am lost in the forest of my false self
I am full of my own opinions and narrow attitudes
   full of fear, resentments, control
   full of self-pity, and arrogance.
Slowly this terrible truth
   pierces my heart
I am so full there is no room for you.

Contemplatively, and with compassion
   you ask me to reach into my water jar.
One by one, Jesus, you enable me

to lift out the things
that are a hindrance to my wholeness.
I take each one to my heart and
I hear you asking me,
"Why is this so important to you?"

Like the murmur of a gentle stream
    I hear you calling,
    Let go, let go, let go!
I pray with each obstacle
    tasting the bitterness and grief
    it has caused me.

Finally. . .
I sit with my empty water jar
I hear you whisper,
    You have become a space for God
    Now there is hope
    Now you are ready to be a channel of life.
You have given up your own agenda
There is nothing left but God.
                    (Prayer inspired by John 4:28)

The Prayer of the Storm

Lord, I'm praying for a storm tonight
One of your very wildest kind!
Oh let it sweep across my ego-self
and empty me. . .
Send lightning flashes bright enough
to charge my tired hope
And let the thunder be so loud
it scares all apathy away.

Lord, open up your clouds
And drench me with your rain
Let this healing flood absolve me

Baptize me once again.
May this downpour from your heavens
refresh my wearied soul
And give me strength for swimming
but let me see the shore.

Lord, I beg you for a storm tonight,
the wildest that you own!
Oh let your winds awaken me
And shake me to the bone.
Lord, do not calm these seas tonight
just be present in the storm.
Sweep across my desert places
and leave them moist with you
Disturb me with a storm tonight
so I'll be born anew.

Prayer Before a Burning Bush

Holy, holy, holy
Lord, God of heaven and earth:

What is this crackling sound I hear,
    this sudden warmth I feel?
    and now, a small flame
    I do not understand!

O God of splendor
You are feeding me mysteries again
You are creating a new fire
    another burning bush, unconsumed
    and this one is in my heart.

Yes Lord,
You have my attention
I am standing in wonder and fear

The burning bush has gotten *too close.*
Speak to me out of this new, fiery sign.

Holy, holy, holy
Lord, God of heaven and earth.
                    (Prayer inspired by Exodus 3:2)

A Prayer for Coming Home

O True and Ever-Living God
I repent of all my false and empty gods
I look again into the closets of my life
    my mind, my heart
    to see what rules me.
Whom do I serve?
What are the possessions
    the people, the opinions
    the events,
    that control my life?

O Welcoming One
I see you standing at the door
    of my heart
    waiting for me
You gaze at my strange gods
    with an eye of compassion.

I am ashamed to invite you
    into my cluttered house
    yet my heart aches
    to be at home with you

My hand is reaching for the door
I hear myself saying, Come on in
I have more room than I thought I had
Come on in, and be the *only* God in my life.
May this moment of homecoming last forever.

Prayer Before an Empty Tree

Jesus
You move through each season
  with your magic wand
One by one
  you have taken my leaves from me
I am the story of your emptiness
You have told me well.

The part of me that feels stripped
  cries out to you,
  "How can I give shade
  with so much gone?"

Again I feel your magic wand
You speak to me of an inner shade
  whose name is peace
  the gift that comes from letting go.
Your story continues to be told in me.
Your story continues to unfold in me.
And suddenly,
  when I look again
  I realize that
  what you have taken from me
  has only made me free
  to see.

I am your story of glory!

A Prayer of Yearning for the Truth

God, forgiving God
My David-heart is crying
  for the truth.

But the truth
  is hard for me to bear:
I have slaughtered other's lambs
and saved my own.
Since the beginning of my days,
I have taken what belongs to
others
  in subtle, hidden ways.

God, forgiving God,
Send me a prophet!
My David-heart
  is crying out for you.
I'm looking for a Nathan
  to bring me down
  with truth.

Send me a prophet, Lord
  to stir up what is settled in me
  to reveal what is concealed.
I'm looking for a Nathan
  to feed me with the truth.

Standing on Tiptoe

The SEASON of HOPE

S tanding on tiptoe is not a children's game of balance. Rather, it is the beautiful prayer of balancing God's promises with my joyful expectation. It is the Season of Hope! I am God's Story of Hope.

The Christian heart has a built-in urgency to expect good things. And why not? We have been promised so much:

- eternal life
- a dwelling place in the heavens
- living water
- answered prayers
- healing and forgiveness
- resurrection
- freedom that comes from knowing the truth
- sacramental life for our journey homeward
- the Spirit
- a new heart.

It is no wonder, then, that in spite of all the brokenness of our lives, we are still standing on tiptoe waiting for the glorious freedom promised us as children of God. This confident waiting is called hope, and our lives are empty without it. It is a small seed that grows wildly when it is nurtured. We cannot teach someone to hope. We give hope by living out of our own hope. We give hope by eagerly awaiting the blessings that have been promised us.

The following meditations are intended in some way to bear the theme of hope. They speak of:

- birth
- Christmas and Jesus
- eager expectations

- epiphanies
- affirmation
- morning
- yeast and rising
- divine presence
- invitations to belief.

In the midst of all these promises you are encouraged and challenged to keep standing on tiptoe. Your joyful expectation might be just the healing ointment needed to minister to someone's tired hope.

Hoping in Darkness

It appears to me that whatever we suffer now will show up only dimly when compared to the wonders God has in store for us. It is as though all creation is standing on tiptoe longing to see an unforgettable vision, the children of God being born into wholeness.

Although creation is unfinished, still in the process of being born, it carries within a secret hope. And the hope is this: A day will come when we will be rescued from the pain of our limitation and incompleteness and be given our share in a freedom that can only belong to the children of God.

At the present moment all creation is struggling as though in the pangs of childbirth. And that struggling creation includes even those of us who have had a taste of the spirit. We peer into the future with our limited vision, unable to see all that we are destined to be, yet believing because of a hope we carry so deep within.

(Romans 8:18–25 [a paraphrase])

Romans 8:18–25 gives us the beautiful vision of creation straining forward, on tiptoe, eagerly waiting for deliverance, for birth, longing to be caught up in God's plan for its wholeness.

Holding this passage up against my own life, I am deeply touched at how personal it has become for me. My own birth into this world began with a proclamation of death. I was proclaimed dead...set aside as *not living*. The nurse, I am told, took me, worked with me, believed in the spark of life in me. She convinced me I could breathe.

Meditating on this story, I am filled with a mixture of anger, tenderness, gratitude, and hope. How easy it would be to throw someone away right in the middle of their birth. I speak not only of that first birth, but of the many ways we are born each day.

Our vision is limited. We need so desperately to learn how to hope more completely in all those little bits of life scattered through our days. We need to be so very careful lest we throw someone away because of our lack of hope in their potential, their possibility to be. We need to believe in that mystery within, even when the mystery seems so pale and small we can hardly call it by its true name, *life*.

This reflection is meant to encourage you to hope. Hope much in the lives of those around you, so that it never need be said of you that someone died because you failed to believe in them.

There was a day in July
many mornings ago
(7:15 A.M. to be exact)
when my hope was so small
I didn't know I was alive.
The doctor placed me aside
and announced the sad news of my death
right in the middle of my birth.

But God was good
and gave someone enough hope
to believe in me.
She leaned forward,
believing in darkness
what some folks refused to believe
in the light.
She believed in me;

and she held me as though
the stirring of the eternal
had just begun,
as though the mystery within
was just being born.

And the joy of it is:
She was right!
Because of her hope in me
I live!

And ever since that day in July
the mystery within me has grown.
The eternal within keeps stirring anew
like a fountain of living water
like a spring that never runs dry.

Could it be true
that some folks die
because our hope is too small
to bring them forth?

It is good to remember:
We do not give birth to ourselves.
We give birth to others
by believing in that first, small spark of life
the spark we can barely see.

It is called hope.
It is immensely helpful
at birth.

The Birth of Christmas

Yahweh spoke to Ahaz again and said: "Ask Yahweh
your God for a sign, either in the depths of Sheol or
in the heights above." But Ahaz said, "I will not
ask. I will not put Yahweh to the test." He then

said: "Listen now, House of David: are you not satisfied with trying human patience that you should
try my God's patience too? The Lord will give you a
sign in any case: It is this: the young woman is with
child and will give birth to a son whom she will call
Immanuel."

(Isaiah 7:10–14)

" . . . Today in the town of David a Savior has been
born to you; he is Christ the Lord. And here is a
sign for you: you will find a baby wrapped in swad-
dling clothes and lying in a manger." And all at once
with the angel there was a great throng of the hosts
of heaven, praising God with the words: "Glory to
God in the highest heaven, and on earth peace for
those He favors." (Luke 2:11–14)

The people in the Old Testament must have lived on
tiptoe. As God moved through their lives they were filled
with the hope of *One who was to come.* They were a people
who waited for promises to be kept and for prophecies to be
fulfilled until at last that day dawned, when they received
the light of revelation. A bright and glorious Word pierced
their darkness. The revelation came in the person of Jesus.
Christmas came to the earth on that day. The Word became
flesh for all who stood on tiptoe.

The following meditations are for folks with Christmas
hearts. They are songs to be sung to an over-commercialized
world, begging its people to remember who Christmas is.

Our autumned hearts stand waiting
for God's gracious gift.
Someone is coming whose sandals
we aren't worthy to carry. (Matthew 3:11)
Prepare the way of the Lord! (Matthew 3:3)

But how do we prepare the way for a King
who is not of this world?
Crowns, red carpets and flowing robes
He desires not at all.

Our ungospelled hearts try to hide
embarrassed at our slowness to respond
to such a gift.

Poor, cluttered hearts
starving for the emptiness
that makes fullness possible
Prepare the way of the Lord!
It is so little that God asks of us.
Give some evidence that you mean to reform. (Matthew 3:8)
Wear lights in your hearts
instead of on your trees.

Our autumned hearts stand waiting
for God's gracious gift
Come, Lord Jesus, come!
Gospel up our lives with your presence
and we'll wear lights in our hearts
instead of on our trees.

Christmas Is for Healing

Weep over your city for Christmas (Luke 19:41–42)
and see if your tears will heal it!

Loving you, of course
I am not at all interested in how much money
you are spending on Christmas gifts this year
but rather, in how much blood, sweat, and tears
you are shedding
to make Christ a vital part of your life
for you and I will never be able to erase

the fact that he came:
   to touch lives—to break bread
   to heal hurt—to forgive sins
   to wash feet—to calm seas
   to walk on water—to give us the Spirit
   and to care immensely

Yes, to care enough
to be born in our Bethlehem
to live in our land, and weep over our cities
and die and rise again.

So now it's Christmas
and I am not sure what part of you is crippled
or where you need to feel God's saving power
but with everything in me
I believe that *Christmas is for healing*
And he came to heal.

So if you can trust Jesus enough to
walk out on the waters of getting involved,
of washing feet and anointing people,
of breaking bread and working miracles,
I am almost sure his saving presence
will touch those blind and crippled parts of your life
and Christmas will come to you.

More than anything else
I want to give you Christmas this year
It's a gift, an offer
You can take it if you like
but I can't really give it to you
like a wrapped up package.
It is deeper than that,
It is warmer, brighter, holier.
It is more personal.
Christmas is more challenging
than a wrapped up package.

It is an offer
It is a mystery
It is birth
It is hope.
It is Christmas and
God can never be born enough...

This offer will not be canceled in case of snow!

Christmas Shopping

O God of words, dear Word made flesh
give birth to my thoughts,
change them into words
that will help me to Christmas up the lives
of those I love, for I am weak and fragile
scared and empty this year
and still I feel you very near.

Jesus, I think I hear you coming
I think I hear a sound that says
you've cared your way into my life again.

I think I see a light more lasting
than the ones we hang on trees
I think I see a world
that's splashed with God again
so gospelled with his presence
so covered with his love
yet, lonely still . . .

O shoppers, dear shoppers
put your carts away.
Please put your carts away
and search deep down within your hearts
for gifts that will not rust or fade
For where your treasure is

there is your heart. (Matthew 6:19–21)
O look into your God-splashed, gospelled hearts
and see! See Christmas standing there
waiting to be, not bought
but given free.

We are Christmas shoppers, Lord
We are shopping for a way
to make your coming last
O take the blind in us and hold it close
O teach us how to see
Decorate our lives with your vision
For Christmas, let us see!

O shoppers, dear shoppers
hang lights in your hearts
instead of on your trees
For the One we've hung our hopes on
has come, and now we're free
but *only if we see.*

Jesus, we long for Christmas-eyes.
Please heal the blind in us
For Christmas, *eyes that see!*

Earthen Vessels

We are only the earthenware jars that hold this treasure, to make it clear that such an overwhelming
power comes from God and not from us. We are in
difficulties on all sides, but never cornered; we see
no answer to our problems, but never despair; we
have been persecuted, but never deserted; knocked
down, but never killed; always, wherever we may
be, we carry with us in our body the death of Jesus,
so that the life of Jesus, too, may always be seen in
our body.   *(2 Corinthians 4:7–10, JB)*

That the Father
trusts us enough
to put the brightness of Christ
into the fragile vessels
that we are
is a Christmas gift
come early.

We are waiting
for someone
we already possess.

We are earthen vessels
filled with a treasure
a Christmas treasure
Christ.
Our earthiness
is only the wrapping
that must be taken off
so that the *gift*
can be seen.

I start early with my unwrapping
I am a slow unwrapper
Sometimes I am gentle with the wrapping
Sometimes I am firm
Sometimes I do nothing but wait.
It takes all,
gentleness, firmness, waiting,
most of all it takes *believing*.
Believing in the treasure
will strengthen the vessel
and yet,
the paradox is this:
We must destroy the vessel
to find the treasure
We must let it be broken
to give it wholeness.

This story will make no sense
except to those
with Christmas-eyes.

On this Christmas
the earthen vessel of me
greets the earthen vessel of you
and prays for a happy unwrapping
for all the earth.

Epiphany

And suddenly the star they had seen rising went forward and halted over the place where the child was.
The sight of the star filled them with delight.

(Matthew 2:9–10)

How often the sight of a star fills us with delight. It is awesome to stand outside and behold a star-studded night. The
stars, it seems, have always called us to greatness. They stir
up within us a sense of mystery. Poets write and sing about
the stars. Artists paint them.

We are told to follow our star. And yet, for all our
romanticizing about the stars, if the truth be known, they
sometimes lead us to places we would rather not go. A star
marks our paths with light and guides us to deeper insight.
With that deeper kind of seeing comes new responsibilities.
It is not always easy to follow a star.

Long ago three who have been called wise journeyed to
the small, insignificant town of Bethlehem. They followed
a star that led them to the powerlessness of God lying in a
manger. It was the last place on earth one would expect to
find the Creator of the stars, yet that is where those beams
did shine. We call such a moment an Epiphany. An Epiph-

any is a manifestation of the Divine Presence right in the midst of daily life.

Those who have tried to follow the Creator of the stars often find themselves in the midst of an Epiphany. They are called to follow stars that seem beyond their reach.

Once a mother whose son had been murdered saw a star that said, "Forgive." The star led her to a prison, to the murderer. The light of the star enabled her to discover within her own heart a mercy she didn't know she possessed. The mercy belonged to the Creator of the stars but it was hers to use when she was in need. She used it well.

There was another woman who had an Epiphany that wouldn't stop. The star she saw shone right into the hearts of the poor. The compassionate ministry that continues in the Catholic Worker houses has turned Dorothy Day into a star that keeps on shining.

Rosa Parks saw a star that shone directly to the front of that bus. She sat there bathed in a bittersweet starlight. It was a difficult Epiphany that bore much fruit.

And what can we say about that prophetic stargazer, Martin? Martin Luther King, Jr., saw a star that is still shining. It was a star of hope for those who were suffering from the oppression and evil of racism and prejudice. He followed that star to his death. He is the patron saint of those who find it hard to follow stars.

And then, there was that man of God from San Salvador. His name? Oscar Romero! He was elevated to the office of archbishop because it was believed he would be a safe, middle-of-the-road person, one who keeps peace by being silent. Perhaps that is who Oscar used to be, but everything changed one day. He had an Epiphany. He saw a star of truth that shone straight through all the lies, impelling him to speak out against injustice. He spoke. He died. His star shines on.

And you? You must add your own names to this list. So many people with hearts of courage have had Epiphanies

that led them to pathways of light. What is your Epiphany?
Where is your sky all shining with stars? And which stars
are calling you?

Creator of the Stars
God of Epiphanies
You are the Great Star
You have marked my path with light
You have filled my sky with stars
    naming each star
    guiding it
    until it shines into my heart
    awakening me to deeper seeing
    new revelations
    and brighter epiphanies.

O Infinite Star Giver
I now ask for wisdom and courage
    to follow these stars
    for their names are many
    and my heart is fearful.

They shine on me wherever I go:
    The Star of Hope
    The Star of Mercy and Compassion
    The Star of Justice and Peace
    The Star of Tenderness and Love
    The Star of Suffering
    The Star of Joy
And every time I feel the shine
    I am called
    to follow it
    to sing it
    to live it
    all the way to the cross
    and beyond

O Creator of the Stars
You have become within me
    an unending Epiphany.

On Being a Star

There are hundreds of stars
    new ones each day
All of them lead to the manger.

We begin small and helpless
    a little piece of clay
    but we grow.

The Potter works at the wheel
The Potter wants us
    to become stars
We become stars
    by following stars
In the eyes of those
    who cannot see
We are fools
    to follow any star
But for those
    with Christmas-eyes
We are wise.

The Potter, too, is a star
The light of this Great Artist
    falls on you
    and you are shaped
    molded
    poured into a Christmas-form.

It takes a long time
    longer than any season

Being born is not easy
    but it's good.
Bless me occasionally
    with your birth.
It heals
    what is frightened in me.

Light shining on light
Of God's radiance
    we have all had a share.
Why else did Jesus come
    except to light a path for us
    to heal what is frightened in us
    and to be a star?

But we aren't used to stars like this
We aren't used to stars
    who are born in a stable
    and hanged on a cross.
We aren't used to stars that shine
    in places we'd rather not look.
We aren't used to stars who propose
    things that don't make sense
    like losing our lives, and
    turning the other cheek
    and being poor for the sake
    of some unknown Kingdom.

I hope a star comes out for you today
A new one that you've never seen before.
I hope it's bright and bold
A prophetic star,
    piercing your darkness
    and helping you to see the things
    you really need to see.

I hope it touches you
    with fire
    and runs along beside you
    all year long.

This star!
Oh, how I hope it comes
    Leaping
    Laughing
    Bounding
    Burning
    Singing
    Shining
        in your life!

And when the year is through
I hope this star
    keeps shining on in you
For without a doubt
    you are
    someone who's called
    to be
    a star.

The Rising

He told them another parable, "The kingdom of
heaven is like the yeast a woman took and mixed in
with three measures of flour till it was leavened all
through."   *(Matthew 13:33)*

It is becoming clear to me that Christians are meant to be a
leaven for our society. We are called to rise in all directions
with the healing presence of our lives. Part of the noble task
of our vocation is to help people discover the hint of eternity

that flows through the inner rivers of their beings. This hint of eternity will nurture their hope. Hope is contagious. Hope is like yeast and baking powder. It has an energy that makes things rise. If you want to know if you are good for others, ask yourself how much hope you've given them. It is there you will find your answer.

I was just thinking
one morning
during meditation
how much alike
hope
and baking powder are:
quietly
getting what is
best in me
to rise,
awakening
the hint of eternity
within.

I always think of that
when I eat biscuits now
and wish
that I could be
more faithful
to the hint of eternity,
the baking powder
in me.

Don't Scare the Dough

Do you not realize that only a little yeast leavens the whole batch of dough? Throw out the old yeast so that you can be the fresh dough . . .

(1 Corinthians 5:6–7)

There are times when we are blessed through remembering. One of the sacred memories that I treasure is my mother baking bread. I would watch her sift and measure the flour. I would watch her kneading the dough. Kneading the dough was a little like loving it she told me. You had to love it just right for it to grow into good bread—not too much, not too little.

While she mixed and kneaded the dough we talked of many things, but when she covered the dough and put it in a warm place to rise, it was time to be quiet and wait. For me, it became a sacred, mystery hour, a holy hour, an hour of watching and waiting for the miracle of rising.

During that time of waiting she would always tell me not to frighten the dough. It seems the dough grew best in a silent, peaceful atmosphere. And so if friends came over to play at that time, I would always tell them: *Don't scare the dough!* They would look at me strangely and never quite seem to understand. But I understood.

Today I understand more than ever. Are we not a little like the dough? Shouldn't we be kneaded just right so we can rise to full stature? And is it not wise for us to give each other a reasonable amount of space, of time, of quiet in which to grow, to rise?

Whenever I make a holy hour I like to compare it to the hour of waiting for the dough to rise. It seems so similar. I sit with the dough of my life waiting for what is unfinished in me to rise. Once again it is an hour of mystery. A hint of eternity steals through my being as I wait for the miracle of rising.

> Dear folks
> make of yourselves
> and of one another
> a fresh new bread
> But don't scare the dough!

Remember
the bread you meet each day
is still rising
Don't scare the dough!

Knead it
Sit with it
Believe in it
Challenge it
Call it forth
Wait for it
Have a holy hour with it
but
Don't scare the dough!

God's Kneading Bowl

So the people carried off their dough, still unleavened, on their shoulders, their kneading bowls
wrapped in their cloaks.

(Exodus 12:34, JB)

I want you to think of yourself as a kneading bowl, a sacred
temple, filled with the dough of your life: your potential,
your gifts, your hopes and dreams, possibilities, all that you
are and can be. God, the Creator, the Loving Midwife is the
Kneader, kneading you to perfection. God is hoping in you.
Experience yourself in those divine hands and rejoice over
who you are becoming.

Think about this especially when you go to the oven of
your heart to wait for your dough to rise. Do not worry at
all about your unfinishedness, your incompleteness. Remember that God is the kneader. Hold that unleavened part
of your life dear and surrender to the energy of your dough.

In higher altitudes the dough rises faster. I do not know what the altitude of your heart is, but be patient with yourself. And when you leave your desert place, leave with hope. Carry off your dough tasting hope as you go.

Becoming overly discouraged about your growth is not healthy. The following meditation was begun in a moment of discouragement. In the middle of my prayer, however, God reached in and showed me the value of my unleavened dough.

> I am leaving the desert
>   with my dough unleavened
>   my kneading bowl carried in my heart.
>
> My journey, so different from
>   that of the Hebrew people
>   who also left with unleavened dough
>   carrying their kneading bowls in their cloaks
> They left in haste
> There was no time for the dough to be leavened
>   no time for the bread to rise.
> They were fleeing from
>   oppression and slavery
>   moving toward freedom.
>
> My journey is so different
> *Pure Luxury!*
> I blush at my carelessness
>   my failure
>   my reluctance to keep vigil with this dough
> I had so much time for my dough to be leavened
>   plenty of time for the bread to rise.
> A beautiful kneading bowl,
>   like a sacred temple
>   was waiting for me:
>   the oven of my heart
>   where God dwells,

Waiting for the dough of my life
  to be given over freely
  to be entered into the wonderful container
    of God's hands,
  to be entrusted to the Divine Potter
    the Great Kneader.

Why then, do I leave here
  with this unleavened dough,
  fleeing from another kind of Egypt,
  fleeing from my unfinished self?

But No, this time my journey is different;
  I am not fleeing.
For the first time in my life
  I am not fleeing.
I came with my unfinishedness
  despairing of it, running from it, afraid of it.
I leave with my unfinishedness
  believing in it, caring for it, embracing it.

I am aware of this unleavened dough of my life
I lovingly embrace it
  and I go slowly; I do not flee
I leave carefully, and aware
  tasting my unfinishedness as I go.
It does not taste like despair
It tastes like hope.
I feel its energy already
I tremble at my potential
It terrifies me still
But I will turn my back on it no longer.

I pick up my kneading bowl,
  which is my entire life in Christ
And I move slowly from this desert place
  tasting hope all the way.

One thing I have learned here:
  If I want to be holy, and
    wholly in God
I must keep vigil always
I must watch with constancy
And I must never flee from what I see
Rather, I must embrace it and say,
"Yes, that's me!"

I continue my journey then, slowly
I carry off my dough
Tasting hope as I go.

A loving God keeps vigil through it all
  reminding me along the way:

  "You must keep yourself
  quietly for me
  and I will do the same
  for you." (Hosea 3:3)

An Amazing Presence

The mystery is Christ among you, your hope of
glory: This is the Christ we proclaim, this is the
wisdom in which we thoroughly train everyone and
instruct everyone, to make them perfect in Christ. It
is for this I struggle wearily on helped only by his
power driving me irresistibly.

(Colossians 1:28–29, JB)

Our human hearts have many questions about the divine.
How do we speak effectively about transcendence in our
modern world? What language do we use when explaining
a mystery? Or can we explain a mystery at all? Do the things
we say flow out of our heart's felt experience or out of a

poured-in head knowledge? How can we be relevant to our modern world without being unfaithful to the authentic proclamation of the gospel?

In any relationship, commitment is crucial. This is no less true of the divine. If we are to have a relationship that is fulfilling and healing, we must be totally committed to this mystery yet always open to new ways of communion.

The following meditation is born of experiences of good in my life. It comes from a presence felt, not learned. It comes from a presence I am unable to explain. It comes from some mystery within me that I have begun to call God.

I am touched to the core
with a presence I can not explain
A loving plan enfolds me
Someone is always believing in me
calling me forth, calling me on
I am standing in grace
filled with mystery
touched with the eternal
I cannot get away from goodness
I think we name you, God.

You surround me like a gentle breeze
My idols live on in my life
My inconsistent values stay
My immaturity walks beside me
My sin is ever before me
Your love for me stays the same
I tremble in the face of such graciousness
Your reverence for me astounds me
You breathe out hope
and I catch on...

Morning, Sacrament of Hope

Dearly beloved: we are not living in the dark, and so
the day will never take us by surprise, like a thief
sneaking into our lives unnoticed. We are children of
light; we are friends of the day. The darkness does
not feel at home with us. Therefore, do not continue
to sleep as those who have no vision, but wake up
and rise with the new day.

(1 Thessalonians 5:4–6 [a paraphrase])

It is easy for me to cry out eagerly with Anne of Green
Gables, "Isn't it a splendid thing that there are mornings?"
There is something so fresh about morning, so utterly new
and untried. Morning is a Sacrament of Hope. She is a gift
of *beginning*. Morning looks at me with eyes of expectancy.
She slips through the darkness on tiptoe.

I like to be awake when morning arrives, ready to be
faithful to the possibility she brings. I want to be waiting for
her, open to receive the gift that she is.

I lean toward the Keeper of Heaven with arms held open
wide. I pray for everyone who, at this moment, is receiving
the gift of morning.

> The East is getting out her gold
> She holds it out against the night
> and scatters darkness
> with her light.
> Then morning comes
> climbing over the hill
> like an eager, restless child.

She pauses just a moment
then casts her color on the earth.

Morning, color me bright
I've been afraid too long.
The color of fear is dark
darker than night
But your glance is full of light.

Don't hurry morning;
come slowly.
Dress yourself in light.
Climb over that hill lovingly
Hand me a new day hopefully
Get into my bloodstream, and
color me like the rising sun
slowly
I've a mind to be contagious
Color me bright.

A Song of Thanksgiving

I thank my God whenever I think of you, and every
time I pray for you all, I always pray with joy for
your partnership in the gospel from the very first
day up to the present. I am quite confident that the
One who began a good work in you will go on
completing it until the Day of Jesus Christ comes. It
is only right that I should feel like this toward you
all, because you have a place in my heart.

(Philippians 1:3–7)

It is important to celebrate with our friends the good things
we see in their lives. Sometimes we forget to affirm the ones
we love most. We take them for granted.

This prayer-song is dedicated to all my friends, with hope that you will sing it to your friends also. Affirmation is a marvelous way of giving others hope.

My heart proclaims a feast
I have come to sing you songs.

I sing of your *warmth*
The steady glow of your friendship
keeps melting the ice in my heart
bringing light to the core of my being
All too often I forget to tell you.
I won't forget anymore!

I sing of your *conviction*
your passion for the truth
Your daring spirit and your boldness
give courage to my fear.
Your thirst for justice
calls forth my hidden prophet.
So often I forget to support you
I won't forget anymore.

I sing of your *gentleness!*
  a strength sometimes hidden
  behind firm convictions
A strength I once couldn't see
  because of my own walls of fear.
Your gift is now out in the light
The veils from my own eyes
  have been lifted.
I celebrate your gift of gentleness
  and encourage you to hold it dear
I once forgot about its home in you.
I won't forget anymore.

I sing of your *conversion*
I celebrate God's love for you
and your constant coming home
    to that love.
I honor your ability to repent
    your willingness
    to examine your heart.
I celebrate your readiness
    to be transformed.

I sing of your *hope*
Your willingness to go on
when all seems to be crumbling
    not with eyes seeing all
    but with expectation of the *promise*.
I celebrate your hope
Your waiting for our God
    to fill up what is lacking in your life.
I promise to be part of your hope
and to stand on tiptoe beside you.
Sometimes I forget you need me there.
I won't forget anymore!

I sing of your *love!*
your life spilled out
that jar of perfume that is *you*
poured out over Jesus
    poured out over me
    and over all who pass your way.
Poured out joyfully at times
    reluctantly at times
But poured out all the same.
I celebrate your love
    your emptying of self
Your life poured out I celebrate.
Sometimes I forget about your love
I won't forget anymore!

And finally, I sing of your *forgiveness!*
  your loving me *anyway*
I celebrate your patience
your patience with my forgetfulness
    my restlessness
    my walls of fear
    my noise
    my empty chatter
    my defenses.

My promise not to forget again
is daring in this moment of recommitment
But my feet are clay.
My heart is broken and scarred in places
In the same heart that I make promises
I break them.
And so, of course, we both know
I'll probably forget again
But I'm not afraid of forgetting
And that's because
I celebrate your forgiveness
    your compassion
    your love
    and understanding.

My heart proclaims a feast
I have come to sing you songs.

A Prayer for Standing on Tiptoe

On tiptoe we stand, Lord Jesus
eagerly awaiting
your full revelation
always expecting you
to come some more.

Our hands and hearts
are open to your grace.
Our lives still waiting for
the fullness of your presence.
We are those who have been promised
a Kingdom, and we can never forget
Yet we have a foot in both worlds
and so we stumble.

But still we stand
on tiptoe
Owning our kingdom-loving hearts
and our earth-eyes
We lean forward
and hope.

Prayer after a Night of Discouragement

God of compassion
Restorer of the Dawn
We know of course

You and I
that morning will,
after this prolonged night,
return.
I've waited before
and never been disappointed
weary, but not disappointed.

Brand your hope
into the center of my heart
just as you once carved me
on the palm of your hand, (Isaiah 49:16)
so that if anyone
should question me
about my hope in darkness
I'll be ever ready to explain. (1 Peter 3:15)

A Prayer to the Potter

Dear Potter,
The lump of clay that I am
keeps crying for some form
day by day
I yearn for you to mold me.

This is a trust-song, Lord
I am in your hands like clay
I am ready to be transformed:

I expect
  to be molded
I expect
  to be beautiful
I expect
  to be loved.

And if by chance
someone should drop me
as your apprentices sometimes do,

I expect
to be hurt.

I'm just trying to say
I have surrendered
to your dream for me
I am in your hands
like clay.

A Prayer to Own Your Beauty

O God
help me
to believe
the truth about myself
no matter
how beautiful it is!

A Prayer for the Body of Christ

God of Hidden Treasures
a time or two ago
I found a treasure hidden in a field
I sold everything I had
ran joyfully
and bought the whole field. (Matthew 13:44)

It is the field that has given me hope,
not just the treasure.
Treasures need a home

a place to rest
to rise, and grow.

Some of the pilgrims with whom I journey
want the treasure
but reject the field.
Yet because of my trust in the field
the treasure has grown.
The field holds all the answers
to the treasure's secret.

God of Hidden Meanings
God of Parables
teach us the wisdom of the treasure
in trusting the field.

The Prayer of One Bursting With Life

Jesus
Tree of Life
Your roots have found me
I am bursting with life
I feel like a brand new bud
singing gratefully to you
I will awaken the world
with the silent song of my being
My voice is not needed
I will preach
the gospel of silence
joyfully
as I burst forth
hopefully
into the sacred space
of this new day
knowing full well

this is only a pale glimmer
of the Life I am becoming
SO FULL OF LIFE AM I!

A Morning Prayer

O Radiant Dawn
O Loving God
as the day begins to tell of your glory
etch into our hearts a bit of heaven
that we may take your shining light
wherever we go.

Shine on us, in us,
and through us
just as your sun shines in the sky.

Give us enough of your light
that we may see the new
GREENING POWER
within us.

Give us
enough lightning and storms
to shake up our soil
enough wind to keep us spirited
enough death to bring us life
and enough goodness
to help us remember who we are.

With trust,
we expect this prayer
to come true in our lives
for it is in the name of Jesus
that we pray.

The SEASON *of* LOVE

The symbolic image of washing feet refers to the ministry that flows out of love. There comes a moment in our lives when we experience the kind of conversion that opens us to new horizons. This conversion will probably reveal certain truths about ourselves and help us to see areas in our lives where we need to change. The sleeping minister in us is awakened, and we begin to discover in our lives resources we never dreamed we possessed. In this awakening moment we come to realize that part of our vocation is to *wash feet*.

This is the Season of Love. What happens in us is the miracle of discovering our potential to care for others. And so, we become a foot-washing, water-walking, healing, beatitude people. Our lives begin *to bless*. We are compelled to respond to the Word of God, to speak in that Holy Name, to live out our ministry of love.

We are fragile vessels whose love often gets tired. We need to be converted over and over again. And so, the healing act of our growth continues. We empty ourselves that we may be filled. We uproot that we may proclaim. We take off our masks. We call forth gifts. We bless. We wash feet. And somewhere between the shedding of our masks and the foot-washing, we discover that it is not so much what we do that touches lives as who we are becoming. And so we rest in the truth that what is most important is not how much of ourselves we leave with others, but how much we enable others to be themselves.

I bless the God who has so often washed my feet. I bless the Christ who has shown me my own potential to be a foot-washer.

The meditations in this section are full of:
· conversions
· blessings
· discarded masks
· discovered gifts
· love poured out.

That's us! God-possessed! Renewed! Tear-filled! Hopeful! Self-emptied! God's Word . . . bursting forth in us!

God in an Apron

When he had washed their feet and put on his outer
garments again he went back to the table. "Do you
understand," he said, "what I have done to you?
You call me Master and Lord, and rightly; so I am.
If I, then, the Lord and Master, have washed your
feet, you must wash each other's feet."

(John 13:12–14)

Try to imagine this scene. You are sitting at the table with
Jesus and his friends on the night before he died. A confusing sorrow overshadows you. Yet, a mysterious hope has
settled in your heart. Suddenly Jesus is standing in front of
you. He looks into your eyes and immediately you are filled
with an awareness of your tremendous worth.

> Supper was special that night
> There was both a heaviness and a holiness
>   hanging in the air
> We couldn't explain the mood
> It was sacred, yet sorrowful.
> Gathered around that table
>   eating that solemn, holy meal
>   seemed to us the most important meal
>   we had ever sat down to eat.
>
> We were dwelling in the heart of *mystery*
> Though dark the night
> Hope felt right
>   as if something evil
>   was about to be conquered.

And then suddenly
the One we loved startled us all
He got up from the table
and put on an apron.
Can you imagine how we felt?

God in an apron!

Tenderness encircled us
  as He bowed before us.
He knelt and said,
  "I choose to wash your feet
  because I love you."

God in an apron, kneeling
I couldn't believe my eyes.
I was embarrassed
  until his eyes met mine
I sensed my value then.
He touched my feet
He held them in his strong, brown hands
He washed them
I can still feel the water
I can still feel the touch of his hands.
I can still see the look in his eyes.

Then he handed me the towel
  and said,
"As I have done
so you must do."
Learn to bow
Learn to kneel.

Let your tenderness encircle
  everyone you meet
Wash their feet
  not because *you have to,*
  because *you want to.*

It seems I've stood two thousand years
    holding the towel in my hands,
"As I have done so you must do,"
    keeps echoing in my heart.

"There are so many feet to wash,"
    I keep saying.
"No," I hear God's voice
    resounding through the years
"There are only my feet
What you do for them
    you do for me."

Would You Mind if I Wash Your Feet?

If Christ should suddenly stand before me with a towel thrown over his shoulder and a pan of water in his hands, would I have the humility to take off my shoes and really let him wash my feet? Or, like Peter, would I say: "Wash my feet, Lord? Never!"

Christ has stood in front of me on many a day. It hasn't always been a pan of water that he's held in front of me, for water is only one symbol of a way to be cleansed and healed. Sometimes he holds a Bible, or sends a letter, or calls me on the telephone. Sometimes she holds a loaf of bread, or a cup of tea, or gives me her shoulder to cry on. Christ comes in so many ways, in so many people, always holding out that basin of water and asking that same embarrassing question: "Would you mind if I wash your feet?"

The beautiful thing about that burning, persistent, foot-washing question is that eventually it calls forth the same question from your heart. Then you discover that your basin is full of water and your heart is full of a call: a call to wash feet.

I discover who I am
  in the act of washing feet
It frightens me to be so powerful
To have so much power and so much grace
  hidden in the mountains
  and valleys of my being
  is scary
I am beginning to suspect who I am
It is so much to be faithful to.

Standing before me
  with a cup of tea in her hands
She revealed to me
  my foot-washing potential
(Would you mind if I wash your feet?)
How about tea every morning at ten?
  she asked.

Sure, I answered
  a little embarrassed
  at being so touched
  by something that simple
It will make ten o'clock sacred
  she assured me.

I nodded in agreement
It was at the right moment she had come
(God always comes at the right moment.)
Nothing had risen in my heart that morning
  and I could tell from her eyes,
  she, too, was waiting for a rising.

It happened simply
  like Jesus washing Peter's feet
We, too, had names
  and we lived them
A few words were exchanged
  over a cup of tea

and, together, we were *the rising*
The action was so simple one could miss it.

It frightens me to be so powerful
  so very full of grace.

Would you mind if I wash your feet?

A Healing Remembered

Finding himself cured, one of them turned back
praising God at the top of his voice . . .

(Luke 17:15)

There are moments when healings take place in our lives and
the only way we can explain the healing is by living it. I've
been reflecting on that one leper, out of the ten, who returned to give thanks to God. I believe the reason he came
back to say thank you is because *he had to*. I think he listened
with all his heart to that healing and was compelled to be
grateful. Reflecting on all the times I've walked away from
God, blessed, I feel like that awakened leper, remembering
my miracle and returning to give thanks.

Many times I walk away from others feeling blessed by
the miracle of their presence in my life. Yet, often, I forget
to tell them. I am convinced that it is only because the Paschal Mystery of many lives has touched the Paschal Mystery
of my own life that I am healed. I celebrate the miracle of
this healing and in the spirit of that grateful leper I proclaim
the following good news:

I used to be shy
I lived inside a lot
Jesus' words fell casually into my life

And soon, I forgot
But then, one day
Jesus struck the rock of my heart (Exodus 17:5–7)
    and I came tumbling out
    singing a new song:

    I'm a gift! I'm a gift!
    I'm God's gracious gift (James 1:16–17)
    My heart is standing on tiptoe
    Jesus just struck the rock of my heart
    And I know I'm God's gracious gift.

Like Jesus, I'm given freely
What do I cost? Not a thing
If you run out of hope, just call me
If you run out of song, I will sing.

If you run out of salt, I'll be flavor (Matthew 5:13)
If you run out of light, I'll be there (Matthew 5:14–15)
If you run out of bread, I will feed you (Mark 6:37)
If you run out of heart, I will care. (Mark 6:34)

Rejoice! You are my sister,
    my brother and my friend (Matthew 12:49–50)
Rejoice! My love is stronger
    than a river without end.
I'll gift you with my presence
I'll color your pain with a song
I'll catch all your tears on my shoulder
I'll heal all your weak with my strong.

I'll walk on the water beside you
I'll hold you if you start to sink (Matthew 14:23–33)
I only ask for your presence
I'm lots more scared than you think.

    I'm a gift! I'm a gift!
    I'm God's gracious gift!
    My heart is standing on tiptoe

Jesus just struck the rock of my heart
And I know I'm God's gracious gift.

Walking on Water

. . .Jesus called out to them, saying, "Courage! It is
I! Do not be afraid." It was Peter who answered,
"Lord," he said, "if it is you, tell me to come to you
across the water." "Come," said Jesus. Then Peter
got out of the boat and started walking toward Jesus
across the water, but as soon as he felt the force of
the wind, he took fright and began to sink. "Lord!
Save me!" he cried. Jesus put out his hand at once
and held him.   *(Matthew 14:27–31, JB)*

There is a resilience in the human heart that borders on
mystery. We have the power to rise, to encourage, to lead,
to dare. It is just such a mood that *walking on water* demands.
If you are bold enough to risk the uncertainty of the waves
I invite you to consider such a walk possible.

Think about what you are most afraid of at this moment
in your life. Then come! Get out of the boat. Walk on the
water with me.

Come, walk on the water with me!
I'm in the mood for impossible things!
Take out your heart of courage,
   a lamp amid your fears
   and walk on the water with me.

Let's touch everything we see
and change it to hope
Our hearts let's change to flesh (Ezekiel 36:26)
No more stones of apathy for us!

Let's look at everything that could be
   believing it *will be*
   if we dare
   to walk on water
   scared and hopeful.

Come, walk on the water with me!
Let's wrap our fears in hope.
Across these waters we must go
   our lamps of courage high
Scared and hopeful we will go.

At the beginning of this water journey
   we'll be careful
   but not too careful.
Being too careful is for the *very* scared.
The Kingdom of Heaven is not found
   in being overly cautious
   but in taking chances.

Come, walk on the water with me!
Hold high your lamp of courage
Put all your doubts away
Let's take a chance on staying up.

Come, walk on the water with me!
I'm in the mood for impossible things.
I feel scared
   because it's impossible
I feel hopeful
   because it's not impossible (Mark 9:24)
So, scared and hopeful
   we will walk.

Come!
Walk on the water with me!

Promises Kept

*. . . never allow your choice or calling to waver;
then there will be no danger of your stumbling, for
in this way you will be given the generous gift of
entry to the eternal kingdom of our Lord and Savior
Jesus Christ.* *(2 Peter 1:10–11)*

In my life there has been an impatient effort to make all
promises permanent experiences. Yet I have failed. My fail-
ure, it seems, would give me boundless patience with others
who find promises hard to keep. Again, I fail. I do not
understand the abandonment that I feel when people walk
away from promises. I stand on the edge of myself. I weep!
I say to myself: Remember all the broken promises of your
own life.

I am one who should have infinite patience with those
who break promises because I've been there so often myself.
I know all about broken promises. They are the banners in
my life that awaken me. They wave in the winds of my life
reminding me to be patient with the broken promises of
others. They ask me to try to understand the pain of so
much brokenness. They ask me to believe in a new promise
that is budding through the brokenness.

This reflection is dedicated to everyone who is struggling to be faithful in relationships. I write these words not
to heap guilt upon those who have broken a promise. That
includes all of us. Yet in a world that is sometimes too casual
about promises these words can be a medicine for the soul.
I am one who believes there is an inner strength in our lives
that we've not yet fully tasted.

Dear friends
Do not lose heart
The Kingdom will suffer if you do.
I, too, am stumbling
   under the burden of
   my not-enoughness.
My unfinishedness cries
   for recognition
   for love
   for acceptance.
My unfinishedness cries
   for wholeness.
It cries for *me!*

There is a promise in me
   that wants to be kept.
It wakes up every morning
   and believes in my faithfulness.
The promise knows that if I break it
   a part of myself will be gone,
   and like water
   running through a cupped hand,
   I may never find it again.

My friends
It is only an illusion
   that our hearts are too weary.
It is only an illusion
   that we are too weak
   to keep promises.
For I know a Kingdom
   that will rejoice forever
   because of *promises kept.*

To Christ Gently

You will have to suffer only for a little while: the God of all grace who called you to eternal glory in Christ will restore you, he will confirm, strengthen and support you. His power lasts for ever and ever. Amen. *(1 Peter 5:10–11)*

To Christ, gently, I sing this song. I was once the most lost of all that is lost. I lived amazingly unconverted. Then one rainy day, under an oak tree, I found myself in an unexpected presence. Jesus washed not only my feet but my heart and my soul. It was a rain of grace. A conversion!

> I am writing this in the rain
> because I love you
> and it was on a rainy day
> you healed me.
> Then having been touched
> by your life,
> I covered my face
> with my heart
> and became *amazingly new*.
>
> I am beautiful at last.
>
> I looked for myself
> in so many places
> and then, in my weariness
> I forgot about myself
> and looked for You.

And behold,
I found myself there
    waiting for me
    in you.

I am beautiful at last.

The Shadow and the Gift

. . . once perfection comes, all imperfect things will
be done away with. When I was a child, I used to
talk like a child, and see things as a child does, and
think like a child; but now that I have become an
adult, I have finished with all childish ways. Now
we see only reflections in a mirror, mere riddles, but
then we shall be seeing face to face.

(1 Corinthians 13:9–12)

Shadows are deceptive. At first glance you think they are
elusive and unreal. But upon examination you discover that
they are miracle-reflectors.

Study the shadow. Let it lead you to its gift. At first do
this experiment out in the sunshine with ordinary, everyday
gifts: trees, rocks, flowers, people. Then go to the room of
your heart. Let the shadow of pain that you don't understand, the shadow of doubt, confusion, or anger lead you to
the miracle of a hidden gift. I plead with you to try this. It
works.

Wide-eyed and excited
I see the gifts I used to stumble over
Praying with the shadow
I have come to understand it.
Leading me into its secret

it has shown me
that it doesn't lie.
Quietly, it proclaims
the existence
of something deeper
something real.

Study the shadow
and you will find the gift.
With eyes wide open
you can see through the shadow
all the way through
to a deeper truth.

Yes, even shadows
can make you wise
once you've discovered
how to look.
For every shadow
hides a gift.
And because of that
I love shadows.

Love Is Not Blind

Love is always patient and kind; love is never jeal-
ous; love is not boastful or conceited, it is never
rude and never seeks its own advantage, it does not
take offense or store up grievances. Love does not
rejoice at wrongdoing, but finds its joy in the truth.
It is always ready to make allowances, to trust, to
hope and to endure whatever comes.

(1 Corinthians 13:4–7)

Difficult as it may be for us to believe, the seed of this
challenging passage from Paul's letter to the Corinthians is

already living in us. Our hearts are able to love like that. It is a gift that we are free to accept or to reject.

Love is one of the most misused words in our language. It is unfortunate that a word so precious has become so abused. Love is a Word that can become flesh in each of our lives. This fleshed-out Word of Love is a mystery. It is the Mystery of God living and acting in our lives. It is the Mystery of God ministering through our touch, and through our voice. It is God seeing through our eyes.

Love is blind, we like to say, but *no;* Love is not blind. The ego is blind. All it can see is itself. But Love is not blind. Love is pure vision! God, seeing through us! The more we allow God to see through us, the more we will notice a great healing taking place in our world.

As you pray the following poem I ask that you read it through once as it is written. Read it a second time changing *love* to God and changing the pronouns accordingly. Read it a third time changing *love* to your own name and changing the pronouns to fit you. You may find this third reading most difficult of all, though also the most incarnational.

Love is not blind
It can see what microscopes
   have never seen
Love does not need a magnifying glass
It has clear eyes that see forever.

You do not have to be afraid
   in love's presence
You will not be used or taken lightly
You will not be ignored or laughed at
Your goodness will be seen
   with the pure eye of truth.

Love does not need glasses
   though some people who love wear them

Those glasses are to see earth-things
    things that will not last
But love sees spirit-things
    the deep things of God that last forever.

You don't have to be afraid of futility
    in love's presence
Love has a way of filling you up
    yet never smothering you.
Love does not greedily snatch you to itself
It breathes on you and gives you wings
    then lets you free.

Love doesn't tell you how to use your wings
    but it watches while you fly
And because love sees
    it can tell you how your flying
    needs to be improved
    —a little higher
    —a little lower
Love watches
    and it knows
    because it sees.

Love's glance is sometimes gentle
    sometimes stern
To fit your need it falls on you
    like morning dew
    or like a lightening bolt
But it is vision to the very end.
It sees the things we dare not see
    because we are afraid of sight
It sees the things we try to hide
    because we are afraid of light
Love is vision
    and love is not afraid.

Too Small a Love

I tell you, that is why her many sins are forgiven—
because of her great love. Little is forgiven the one
whose love is small.   *(Luke 7:47, NAB)*

When I meditate on the scriptures I would rather not be the
person God is challenging. I don't like to think of myself as
the Pharisee or the one with the hardened heart. This morning as I was praying the beautiful story of Mary washing
Jesus' feet with her tears, I was so sure that I was the *Mary*
of the story. But suddenly God came to me in a way I did
not expect. My comforting prayer turned into a storm, and
I had to acknowledge the unhappy truth that sometimes I
am Simon, the Pharisee, judging others without knowing
the whole truth.

> Like lightning at dawn
> the All-Powerful One came
>   electrifying
>   energizing
>   frightening
>   shattering
>   crashing
> into my morning prayer!
>
> Totally unprepared
>   for this kind of interruption
> I froze on my knees
>   both in wonder and terror.
> There was no morning silence left,
>   no comforting darkness to enfold me

only those flashes of light
that make hiding impossible.

It wasn't exactly a surprise
I was expecting God this morning
but not like this
I was waiting for peace
I was looking for that quiet reassurance
that silence sometimes brings.
I was listening for a sound of wings
hovering over me
surrounding me with care
convincing me of presence and protection.

But this?
Oh, this was awful!
God stood there
with terrible,
penetrating
loving eyes,
saying only:
Your love is too small!

Standing that close to truth
felt uncomfortable, unbearable
and I tried to hide my face
the way I often do
when truth gets too close.
I tried to hide the pieces
of my terribly divided heart.
But then the lightning came again.

And God was standing there
even closer than before
holding the pieces of my heart
with such tenderness
still saying,
Your love is too small.

With that last bolt of lightning
    a great calm came over me
    and I felt free
    the way I always feel, when
I'm finally able to own the truth.

God gave me back the pieces of my heart
without trying to fix them up or mend them
The Holy One looked at me with trust
    with total confidence
    as if to say,
I'll be here when you're ready to begin
    the transformation of your heart
For we both know
Your love is too small
That's why your heart is so divided
That's why the pieces never seem to fit.

I took the pieces back with reverence
My tears proclaiming
    the truth of all I felt.
There was no pressure, no force
    just the God of morning
    asking for my love.

And now, every time I see those flashes
    in the northern sky
I hear again, a voice
    saying simply,
Your love is too small.
And I weep; I weep at the possibility
    of who I could be.

Beatitude People

Seeing the crowds, he went up on the mountain, and
when he sat down his disciples came to him. And he
opened his mouth and taught them, saying:

- Blessed are the poor in spirit, for theirs is the kingdom of heaven.
- Blessed are those who mourn, for they shall be comforted.
- Blessed are the meek, for they shall inherit the earth.
- Blessed are those who hunger and thirst for righteousness, for they shall be satisfied.
- Blessed are the merciful, for they shall obtain mercy.
- Blessed are the pure in heart, for they shall see God.
- Blessed are the peacemakers, for they shall be called sons [and daughters] of God.
- Blessed are those who are persecuted for righteousness' sake, for theirs is the kingdom of heaven.

(Matthew 5:1–12, RSV)

The beatitudes are for people who have their hearts set on the Reign of God. They are a way of life designed for those who want their lives to be a blessing. Beatitude people are kingdom-people. They have a kingdom on their minds that won't let them rest until all the world is striving to be just, compassionate, and single-hearted. They call us forth from the cozy ruts of daily living and urge us to be Christ in the world. They tell us that the Reign of God is already in our midst if we can bless the world with beatitude-living. The beatitudes are values that come straight from the heart of Christ.

In praying with these beatitudes, I tried to image people who were poor and meek, those who were persecuted and hungry for justice and peace. I asked them to tell me their story. Here is the wisdom they shared with me:

Blessed Are the Poor in Spirit, the Reign of God Belongs to You

I turned to the empty ones,
What does it mean to be poor in spirit? I asked
Is there anything good about being that poor?

The poor in spirit replied:
Can God fill anyone who is full?
And how sad if you should suddenly discover
that you are full of illusions
instead of filled with truth.

Being poor in spirit means
having nothing to call your own
except your poverty
It is a joyful awareness of your emptiness
It is the soil of opportunity
For God has space to work
in emptiness that is owned.

Being poor in spirit means
knowing that you are so small
and dependent
needy and powerless
that you live with open hands
and an open heart
waiting to be blessed.
For only then can you be blessed
if you know
that you need blessing.

Being poor in spirit
means that you have time
you are not oppressed by deadlines
There is always time for waiting
for the one who is poor.
Being poor in this way

frees you from the prison
of having to have everything
planned and structured
as though there were no tomorrow.

And finally, being poor in spirit
means being able to say
without embarrassment
humbly, and yet with passion:
"I need you."

Blessed Are You
Who Mourn, Consolation Shall Be Yours

What does it mean to mourn?
I asked those who were sorrowing
An old man stepped forward.

To mourn, he said, is to be given
    a second heart
It is to care so deeply
    that you show your ache in person.

To mourn is to be unashamed of tears
It is to be healed and broken
    all in the same moment.

Blessed are you if you are so full of compassion
    you see the need before it's spoken.
Blessed are you if you can offer to others
    a heart that feels their sorrow
    a heart that can wait quietly beside them
    a heart that doesn't try to hurry the healing.

To mourn is to forget yourself for a moment
    and get lost in someone else's pain
    and then, to find yourself
    in the very act of getting lost.

To mourn is to be an expert
in the miracle
of being careful with another's pain.
It is to stand in solidarity
with the poor and persecuted of the world.
It is to stand in solidarity
with those who cannot help themselves.

To mourn is to join the song of the dying
and to be healed
by the song
and the death.

Blessed Are You Who Are Meek, You Shall Have the Earth for Your Inheritance

And to the meek, I said:
Tell me about this beatitude
It doesn't sound like a blessing
To me, it looks like the face of weakness.

A face out in the crowd of lowly ones
shone forth with strength
Her smile reached the door of my heart.
Then this lowly one spoke,

To be meek is to be so full of truth
that everyone is comfortable
in your presence.
It is to have a spirit young as the dawn
a heart old as the evening.
It is to know yourself so well
and live yourself so fully
that your very presence
calls forth gifts in others.
It is to be comfortable
with your anger
and with your compassion.

The meek one grew silent for a moment.
Then lifting her eyes, she said:

When you are meek
you don't need a lot of followers
you just need a lot of truth.

The lowly ones are able
to stand out in the open
and speak the truth
   sometimes quietly
   sometimes loudly.
The truth will be spoken
   even if no one listens
   even if no one hears.
For the meek person doesn't need followers
The meek need to be true to themselves.

No greater truth was ever spoken.
The meek shall inherit the earth.

Blessed Are You Who Hunger and Thirst for Justice: You Shall Be Satisfied

But what is justice? And what is righteousness?
And who is that hungry?
I cried out to the whole world.

We are, the people called back.
We have spent all our money
  on things that don't last.
We are hungry with a hunger that is deep inside.
We are hungry with a hunger that won't be silent.
We are hungry for something whose name is
   everything virtuous
   everything noble
   everything true.

We are hungry for all that matters
   for all that is lasting
   for all that is right.
We are hungry for
   broken bread
   and answered prayers
   and kept promises.
We are so hungry
   cried the people.

Then trembling beneath the burden
   of such a hunger, I asked:
What have you done to your prophets?
The people grew silent
and the silence became a song.

Then someone stepped out of the crowd.
We are too sophisticated
   to stone our prophets, he said
   and so we just ignore them
   and our hunger deepens.
If you are wondering what to pray for
We are hungry for new hearts.

I bowed my head in the city streets
And I wept with grief and joy
I announced Good News
   to all who would listen
   and the news was this:

Blessed are you if you are aware
of so deep a hunger
for God will surely feed you.

And then everything tired in me
   leaned against everything strong
   and I cried out
Show me the face of mercy.

And the merciful ones answered
You are most like God
   when you are dressed
   in the robes of mercy.
Mercy doesn't judge; it loves.

And the merciful ones continued,
We are the merciful
We are standing at every pathway
   ready to heal what needs healing
   ready to forgive what needs forgiving.
Compassion is our way of life
Forgiveness is our pastime.
We throw it around unconditionally
   like dew on summer grass
   like rain on dry, parched earth.

We are those who have been forgiven
   while still guilty
And we can never forget.
Forgiveness has touched
   every fiber of our lives
And so we spend our lives *forgiving*.

Then everything tired in me
   stood up tall,
Hope returned and I asked:
Could you forgive even me?
I have been so careless with God's love
I have cared for myself before others.

Then someone from the crowd stepped forth
She touched me with her presence as she spoke:
"God's care is greater than your carelessness
Go in peace, Your sins are forgiven."

An overwhelming desire to forgive
    began to thread its way through my soul
Standing on the threshold
    of my human frailty
It gazed into the depths
    of my soul
    and became
    the *Mercy of God.*

Blessed Are the Pure of Heart, You Shall See the Face of God

With deep reverence
I turned to the pure of heart,
How does it feel to be pure of heart? I asked.

With simplicity
One with a pure heart replied:

It feels like a child exploring a new day
It feels like all your false idols have tumbled
    as you stand amid ruin and creation
    with brand-new eyes.
It feels like having eyes
    that do nothing but *see*
    and all things are possible
    for those who can see.

To be pure of heart
    is to be transparent
It is to have a heart that doesn't hide,
    an undivided, single heart
    a heart that feasts

on the *one thing necessary:*
life in and of God.

To be pure of heart
is to have a heart
with direction
expectation and purpose.

It is to seek first
the reign of God
believing all else
will be given it besides. (Matthew 6:33)

To be pure of heart
is to be free.

Blessed Are the Peacemakers, *You Shall Be Called Children of God*

Then all the violence in me
cried out to the peacemakers:
But where do you get all the peace
that you share?

An old woman answered:
We give best what we are
she said,
I have searched deeply
into the mystery of myself
for something that would last
through all the storms of life.
I have waited in faith
for a great healing
to arise within me.
I prayed that when it came
I would recognize it
welcome it home
and then give it away

For we can only keep
  what we give away.

And now
  this long awaited star
  has risen in my heart
It's name is *peace.*

I found it waiting for me
  deep inside
  on the day I stopped looking
  and started seeing.

And now, more than anything
  that needs to happen
  in the human heart
I long to help it see the peace
  that's already there.

I am the peacemaker
I make peace by showing you my star
  and leading you to see
  the space for God you are.

Blessed Are Those Who Are Persecuted for Being Christ, the Reign of God Is Yours

I felt an anger welling up inside of me
  and in my bewilderment, I asked:
How could the persecuted feel blessed?

And the persecuted ones replied:
Why should we not drink this cup?

The suffering that is most fulfilling
  is the one that comes
  from standing by the side
  of those who have no power.

It is not the suffering
  that we love so much
It's the peace that comes
  from protecting what we cherish.
There is no joy
  like the joy of being a voice
  for the voiceless.
There is no peace
  like the peace that comes
  from speaking the truth.

For when conviction
  screams inside of you
  to let it live
When everything you stand for
  and everything you believe in
  become a song in you,
Then dying's not so hard at all.

Blessed are you if you can believe
  that deeply.
Blessed are you if you can care
  that passionately.
Blessed are you if you can love
  like Jesus.

Yes, He came to cast a fire on the earth
  and I am almost certain
He expects us to be part of the kindling.

Blessed are you if can suffer persecution
  for the cause of right.
Blessed are you if can care that much
  and die that well
  and be that free
The Kingdom of heaven is yours!

The Prayer of the Beatitudes

O Christ of the Poor in Spirit
They have no light of their own
  no wealth of their own
Yet because of your glory
  shining within them
  they will be known in the Kingdom of God.
O Christ of the Poor in Spirit
Create in my crowded heart
  a space for God.

O Christ of Those Who Mourn
A holy sorrow washes my soul
  as the ache of others' pain
  threads its way through my being.
Sharing their sorrow
  without trying to take it away
  brings healing and comfort.
O Christ of Those Who Mourn
Create in me a new courage
  to sit beside the sorrowing.

O Christ of the Lowly Ones
Possessing no power
  save a truth deep within,
God's anawim★ linger long
  over that truth.

★poor little ones

They receive
    rather than take.
O Christ of the Lowly Ones
Create in me a gentle, open spirit.

O Christ of Those Who Hunger for Justice
What is this gnawing in the center of their being?
Hunger-pains, refusing to be satisfied
    with anything less than God.
In the deep caverns of their souls
    lives a blazing zeal
    that burns for righteousness.
O Christ, Sun of Justice
Burn your way into my soul
    with the terrible gift
    of this same blazing zeal.

O Christ of the Merciful
Who are these people
    wearing the robes of your mercy?
Have you returned again
    in the person of their flesh?
Your love shines out in them
    like a full moon.
O Christ of the Merciful
Dress me in the warm robes of your mercy.

O Christ of the Pure of Heart
Who are these fearless ones
    seeing with their hearts
    calling me to connect
    with my own God-like heart?
In the center of my being
    dwells a heart that is *one,*
    a stranger to division.
Forever it whispers,
    I am already within you.

Believe in me! Believe in me!
O Christ of the Pure of Heart
Create in me a deep faith
   in an undivided heart.

O Christ of the Peacemakers
Who are these dreaming dreams
   carrying torches
   building bridges?
They walk in peace
   out where the wild things are.
They pitch their tents
   in fields of violence
And all of this
   because they are at peace
   within themselves.
O Christ of the Peacemakers
Create in me a peaceful heart
   that cannot stay at home.

O Christ of the Persecuted
Twisted, broken,
   bent upon the cross
   they proclaimed all the truth they knew.
They died of truth, and
   the Kingdom of Heaven became theirs.
O Christ of the Persecuted
Create in me a willingness
   to die for the truth.

A Prayer for Washing Feet

Jesus
Is it really you
   kneeling before me
   with that bowl of water
   in your hands?

I'd feel more comfortable
     if we could trade places
I wouldn't mind kneeling before you,
     but you before me?
I can't let you love me that much.

Your piercing eyes
     suddenly
     heal my pride.
I'm able to accept
     your gift of love
     and I am blessed.

O Gift Giving God
I blush
with the memory
of gifts I've refused
because they weren't given
my way.

A Prayer for Growing Up

My Lord
Why do I storm heaven
for answers
that are already in my heart?
Every grace I need
to love folks well
has been given me
needing only my response
my willingness to let your grace
grow up in me.

Jesus,
Lead me to the grace-filled shores
of myself rooted in you

for it is there you have made your home.
Wash these wayward feet of mine
Water the seeds you have planted.
O Lead me to the *beyond* within.

Prayer for a Tired Branch

Jesus
I am one worn-out
tired branch
and I need the newness
of the vine of you
to start the hope-life
running through
the streams of me again.
Lord, be my vine
and I'll be your branch
but free me please
from this withered
cut-off feeling
and deliver others
from the pain
I carve into their branches.

A Prayer for All Good Gifts

Jesus, giver of all good gifts
On this barefoot journey
I stand in constant need of foot washing
Carrying your promise in my heart (Matthew 7:7)
Pilgrim that I am, I plead for help along the way:

For the gift of *vision*
that I may see with heaven's eyes
so that people will be safe in my presence.
    Give me your vision.

For the gift of *conviction*
that I become the song of the gospel
Your Word made flesh in me.
    Give me your conviction.

For the gift of *compassion*
that I may always be a healing presence
bending low to wash feet and touch wounds.
    Give me your compassion.

For the gift of *poverty*
that I may be at home with emptiness,
a willing space for God.
    Give me your poverty.

For the gift of *stability*
that I may be able to stay with the gospel
in times of discouragement.
    Give me your stability.

For the gift of *hope*
that I may stand on tiptoe with the whole world
waiting for rebirth, growth, completion.
    Give me your hope.

For the gift of *reverence*
that I may hold sacred the gift of each person,
ever proclaiming the value of all creation.
    Give me your reverence.

Finally I pray for the grace
to *recognize* each gift as it is given,
receive it as gift
and acknowledge it as mine to give away.
    Give me your own self-giving.

The SEASON *of* MYSTERY

The race to the tomb surprises me more than any other kind of walk in life. The surprise centers around an ancient belief of mine that needs to be rearranged. The race to the tomb, for me, has always meant death. Yet, in my own acting out of this race, I find it difficult to separate death from life. It seems that when you welcome death as one of the necessary breaths to be drawn, it changes before your very eyes into life.

I say this not only of that sacred moment when we step into eternal life, but also of my daily sacred moments that are filled with this same truth.

It is the way of all the earth! Each breath of life is given to us as a gift from another's death breath. At every moment something or someone is sacrificing life to give life. Our race to the tomb, then, becomes a symbol of an emptiness that must be embraced if we are ever to understand life. Arriving at the tomb, the surprise that awaits us is that emptiness and death have been changed into life. Each meditation in this section proclaims the glory of the sacrament of death and life.

The race to the tomb means losing life. It means finding life. It means wheat falling into the ground and dying, only to rise again. It means life dug out of death, joy born out of pain. It means racing to the tomb, discovering the surprise of all surprises: *life!*

Easter—Gift from the Tomb

Since you have been raised up to be with Christ,
you must look for the things that are above, where
Christ is, sitting at God's right hand. Let your
thoughts be on things above, not on the things that
are on the earth, because you have died, and now
the life you have is hidden with Christ in God. But
when Christ is revealed—and he is your life—you,
too, will be revealed with him in glory.

(Colossians 3:1–4)

Suddenly, all my hidden life proclaims a feast and Easter arrives. Easter comes after the sleep and death of winter and after the struggle of Lent. It comes, as it did for Peter and John, after my race to the tomb. It is one more sign of the way death and life stand side by side and seem to slide over into each other, becoming *one* just at the moment when I reach the tomb and peer in to see if Jesus is present or absent. As is often the case, sometimes God's absence feels like presence; and sometimes the Divine Presence feels like absence.

We will be racing to the tomb as long as we live. We will be peering into the tomb of our hearts to see if Jesus is really there. At moments like this it would be grace if we could be given the gift of simplicity and authentic grief. Perhaps then, in our moment of uncertainty, we, like Mary, would remember to check with the gardener (John 20:14–16), and the mystery of death and life would be solved.

Our willingness to remove all stones from the doorways of our tombs is important if we wish to find the hidden life in us. If we are willing to become actively involved in this stone-rolling process, our inadequate and unwhole lives become filled with new life, and celebration becomes absolutely essential.

When celebration is the only thing that makes sense, we have begun to understand the sacredness of life and death. The meditations that follow have been written near the tomb.

Racing to the Tomb

So Peter set out with the other disciple to go to the tomb. They ran together, but the other disciple, running faster than Peter, reached the tomb first; he bent down and saw the linen cloths lying on the ground, but did not go in. Simon Peter, following him, also came up, went into the tomb, . . . Then the other disciple who had reached the tomb first also went in; he saw and he believed. Till this moment they had still not understood the scripture, that he must rise from the dead. The disciples then went back home.   *(John 20:3–10)*

On a morning that felt like Easter,
   in the spirit of Peter and John
   I raced to the tomb.
All those who have come to depend on me
   and I on them
   seemed to be racing with me.
They got there first,
   but waited,
   too reverent to enter without me.

Peering into my baptized heart,
   my tomb
   where my life is hidden

with Christ
in God
I entered
with resurrection on my mind.

Those who raced with me
followed me in
always waiting
for me to make the first move.
Waiting and watching
for the dough of my life to rise
companioning me in the rising.

How difficult it is to rise alone
And such a comfort
when someone waits with you
for the rising.

What is the sense
of Jesus having risen 2000 years ago
if I cannot put my linens aside
and claim resurrection
as my own
today!

The problem came
when my friends had to go away
to race with someone else
to the tomb.
I began to doubt my rising
and started to cling
to the linens again.

But I was lucky enough
to run into the gardener,
and Mary's question
became my own,
Where *is* the One I love? (John 20:14–16)

My name, proclaimed
   became my answer!

Now I, too, can race with others to the tomb
   allow them to enter first
   and wait with them
   for the rising.

On Rolling Stones Away

And very early in the morning on the first day of
the week they went to the tomb when the sun had
risen.
   They had been saying to one another, "Who will
roll away the stone for us from the entrance to the
tomb?" But when they looked they saw that the
stone—which was very big—had already been rolled
back.   *(Mark 16:2–4)*

Where are my stones?
What are their names?
Would I know them
   if I met them face to face?

And if the empty tomb
   I stood in front of was *me*
   would I call it death?
Or would I call it resurrection?

My heart beats out the answer
much clearer than I live it.
O happy emptiness!
It's what I need a lot of
to be full.

Rolling stones
is what it's all about
but Resurrection
is another name.

> Be patient with each other's stones
>   (Ephesians 4:1–3).
> Jesus was gentle with Thomas' stone
>   (John 20:24–29).
> Peter had to roll away some stones in his life too
>   (John 13:6–11).

The call continues.
We are called
to help others experience Resurrection
to help them break out of their tombs.
Of course, that means
we'll have to break forth
from our own tombs first.

We'd look kind of silly
preaching
from the inside of our tombs,
wouldn't we?

On Letting Easter In

After the Sabbath, and toward dawn on the first day
of the week, Mary of Magdala and the other Mary
went to visit the sepulcher. And suddenly there was
a violent earthquake, for an angel of the Lord, descending from heaven, came and rolled away the
stone . . . the angel spoke; . . . "There is no need
for you to be afraid. I know you are looking for
Jesus who was crucified. He is not here, for he has
risen, . . . go quickly and tell his disciples, 'He has

risen from the dead and now he is going ahead of you to Galilee; that is where you will see him.' Look! I have told you." Filled with awe and great joy the women came quickly away from the tomb and ran to tell his disciples. And suddenly, coming to meet them, was Jesus.

(Matthew 28:1–9)

On Easter morning should you be surprised to find Jesus coming to meet you? But what if you didn't know it was Easter? What if there had never been an Easter morning before? What if it was the day after the most sorrowing day you had ever experienced, the day after that painful Sabbath when he had lain in the tomb, dead? Dead as your hopes and dreams! Dead as your joy! Dead as the life you once felt!

Is it so amazing then—this trembling awe we felt? We came to the tomb to find him dead as our hearts, but an angel was there with a story of *life*. If you're wondering what Easter really is—it's finding leaven in a dough that was dead. It is despair moving over to make room for hope. It is joy suddenly crowding out your sorrow. It is a tomb transformed into a womb—life pushing its way out of death. It is the stone being rolled away on the morning of a great sorrow. The angel of life at the tomb of death!

When dawn stands still with wonder
when birds jubilate in the trees
when buds hurry into blossoms
and grass starts wearing green
I always know that Easter wants to come again.

But deeper yet and richer still
When Jesus, imprisoned in me,
asks me to roll away the stone

that locks him in
then Easter wants to come again.

So, let it come
It's one dawn past rising time
and Resurrection is the wildest news
that's ever touched
this crazy, mixed-up world.
It says, *yes!*
when everything else says, *no!*
It says, *up!*
when everything else says, *down!*
It says, *live!*
when everything else says, *die!*

Easter's standing at your door again,
so don't you see that stone has got to go?
that stone of fear
of selfishness and pride
of greed and blindness
and all the other stones we use
to keep Jesus in the tomb.

So here's to rolling stones away
to give our Lord the chance He needs
to rise and touch
a troubled, lonely world.
Some call it *Resurrection.*
It's wild with wonder,
It's beautiful and real
Intent on throwing life around
it touches and it heals!

Yes, Easter, you can come
An angel of life I'll be.
I'll roll the stone away
and set you free.

An Ode to Life

Death, where is your victory? Death, where is your
sting?   *(1 Corinthians 15:55)*

What happened to death?
How terribly gone it is!
All the world is filled with *Life* today
For someone stepped on death
and Resurrection happened!

Someone stepped on death
and *Life*
    leaped out
    leaped up
    leaped in.
A friend named Life walked in!

Welcome, Life!
It's been a long, hard winter,
  and a crucifying Lent.
The welcome that you feel is real.

We call you *Life*
Oh what a gift you are!
You breathe in us and make us new
You stroll among our doubts
You walk amid the pain
Even sin cannot destroy you.

As you stand beside us
with resurrection eyes
death itself, now, dies.

Patience, Life!
One secret at a time.
Too much beauty we can't manage
Too much mystery overwhelms us.
    Go gently then
    as you touch us with your breath
    a little more each day
    and then again some more
    until we're *new*
    and *full of you.*

Then,
we can be
life-giving
too!

Communion

Something which existed since the beginning,
which we have heard,
which we have seen with our own eyes,
which we have watched
and touched with our own hands,
the Word of Life—
this is our theme.   *(1 John 1:1)*

This Word who is Life has made a home in all living crea-
tures. All that is alive draws life from this Word. When I am
in communion with Life I am in communion with God.

There are moments of communion when I find it hard
to stay in my body, moments when the God in nature becomes so intimate my spirit feels pulled to a deeper realm.
At moments like this I pray. I turn toward the object of my
devotion and become radically present to it. This is prayer.

One such prayer I celebrated with an evergreen tree on a rainy day in Oregon. Our communion went something like this:

Evergreen tree,
don't mind if I rest for a moment
Allow me to sit under your evergreen roof
and think evergreen thoughts for a while
A thought is as green as you make it.

Hello, green thought!
I see you're made of *life,*
the best thing to be made of on a rainy day.
Life doesn't melt in rain
It just hangs around and grows!

Grow me up, life!
Sift your gentle greenness through me
till we're hard to tell apart, and then
let's run through all this human traffic together.
Let's bump into people
and perk up their tombs
greenly . . .

Leftover Sun—Leftover Transcendence

And so we have no eyes for things that are visible,
but only for things that are invisible; for visible
things last only for a time, and the invisible things
are eternal. *(2 Corinthians 4:8, JB)*

Transcendence is elusive, just like the sun! The sun comes to the end of my day and just when I think I own it, it's suddenly gone. But, oh, the footprints it leaves in the sky! Only a happy sky could hold such glory. Then night falls, and I wait for morning.

Isn't my life a little like the sky? As untouchable for sure! My life holds transcendence like the sky holds the sun. And I am almost certain on some days, if you would look me in the eye you would see in me as much leftover transcendence as the sky has leftover sun.

> the sun
> comes climbing down
> the mesquite tree
> with thoughts of escaping
> into the buffle grass
> and i watching with love
> delight in its flight
> knowing that its parting gift
> will be a flaming sky
> all excited with
> leftover sun
> and morning will find me
> on the other side
> sitting beside the purple sage
> waiting for it to come once more
> climbing
> over the buffle grass
> the sun.

> a god
> steps quietly
> out of my life
> wanting to be sure
> i am not crippled
> with dependency
> and i watching with love
> receive the dark night of my soul
> my life still ablaze with
> leftover transcendence

and morning
will find me
after my soul's dark night
waiting
for a god
to step quietly
back into my life
a god.

On Beauty and Treachery

I cannot understand my own behavior. I fail to carry
out the things I want to do, and I find myself doing
the very things I hate. . . . In fact, this seems to be
the rule, that every single time I want to do good it
is something evil that comes to hand. In my inmost
self I dearly love God's law, but I can see that my
body follows a different law that battles against the
law which my reason dictates. This is what makes
me a prisoner of that law of sin which lives inside
my body.   *(Romans 7:15–23, JB)*

There is such a fine line between life and death, good and
evil, beauty and treachery. The power in any one of these,
slightly rearranged, could mean a blessing or a curse. I have
never understood this closeness. It is part of the mystery of
our lives. At times it is frightening; at times it is reassuring.

It is my hope and prayer that the treachery hidden in all
of our hearts will be overpowered by the beautiful. I am one
who constantly experiences the struggle between the two.

I'm for beautiful things
like
lightning and hailstones

and
storms and people!

And
I'm for treacherous things
like
lightning and hailstones
and
storms and people!

I'm for life
with all its faces.

White ice balls
they come
pounding through the puzzled air
dancing on the waiting earth
fairies from the sky
and
one of beauty's faces.

But
the wheat is sad
and large and lovely purple grapes
try to hide
but can't.

The farmer's face is saddest of them all
He stands and watches
and remembers
the work he did
for fruit he'll never see.

But
I'm for life
with all its faces.

And storms come too
They never ask, just come
bringing
their wild and wondrous winds

with thunderclaps
and lightning flashes
big, godlike, golden flashes
that sometimes kill
another face of life.

And people?
the most beautiful
and treacherous of all!
No hailstone
no storm with angry winds
no flash of lightning
can dig its claws so deep
or hurt so well
Nor can they smile with graciousness
or open up their hands
and dig down deep within
and give
so well!

Beautiful?
Yes!
But sometimes they kill.

Unless . . .

In all truth I tell you, unless a wheat grain falls into
the earth and dies, it remains only a single grain; but
if it dies, it yields a rich harvest.

(John 12:24)

I gaze lovingly at my dinner plate filled with gifts from the
earth. I am touched, overwhelmed at the truth that everything I eat has in some way had to die so I could live. It is
the way of the earth, and I do not completely understand it.

Ponder over that truth for a while. It may bring tears to your eyes. And if it does, I encourage you to welcome them. They could be healing.

I gaze more lovingly still. Gratitude overflows! I ask my heart a hard question: What is it in me that must die before I can truly give life to others?

Lord, you have made me for Life
but I fail.
When the pale, gray uncertainty of the unknown
smothers me
I grow afraid inside,
so afraid.
I refuse the gift of the unknown.
Grasping for life I become deadly.
From my tiny world I lean forward
crying as though there is some Egypt
I need to be delivered from.
It is the Egypt of my imprisoned self
crying out within me
begging me to let it die
so others can live.

Oh! being life is not easy, folks.
it is not easy until
I can free it from its prison
by being death,
by dying for it well
so well!

Unless
a grain of wheat
falls into the ground
and dies
it remains just a single grain
but if it dies

it yields
a rich harvest.

Unless . . .

The Coming of Truth

"If you make my word your home you will indeed
be my disciples; you will come to know the truth,
and the truth will set you free."

(John 8:31–32)

Truth has a way of showing up our lies. Sometimes we keep
the sin in our lives well protected, guarded, covered over
with lies. Sometimes we are not free enough to own our sin,
so we cannot be healed of it. An unacknowledged wound
cannot be healed.

Truth has a way of waiting for us to come forth and
confess the lies of our lives. It has a way of gazing at us until
we can bear the look of truth no longer. It is then we receive
grace to turn to truth and welcome it home. Only when we
welcome truth does it have the power to color our lives with
honesty.

The truth stands waiting
in my lie-filled life
On the edge of myself it stands
and looks without interruption
into my sin-filled heart
and everywhere its glance falls
I am dying all the while.

I have needed to die for so long!

O Lord, God of life and death
thank you for this life-giving death

for this piece of sin
that I can own
and claim at last
and not deny.
It's mine!
Mine to weep over
and acknowledge
and die to
and give to you.

I am dying at last
Truth is falling through my life
like lightning
I am losing my life
I am finding my life.

Amen, My Lord, Amen!

So by our baptism into his death we were buried
with him, so that as Christ was raised from the dead
by the Father's glorious power, we too should begin
living a new life.   (Romans 6:4)

At baptism I was invited to say Amen with my life. A community who loved me and carried faith in their hearts said
that first Amen for me. But we cannot live our lives on
other people's Amens. There comes a day in each of our
lives when we have to decide if we are ready to say our own
Amens. And so, the day dawned in my life when I felt called
to take my community's Amen and make it my very own.
I said *yes*, on that day, to the event of my baptism. *Yes*, to
all of the death and life it would ask of me. "Baptism," I
said, "is exactly what I want. I'll never take it back."

Having accepted that invitation, my life's Amens keep singing in my heart, and because I love you I want to share both the struggle and the joy of this Amen with you.

Amen, my Lord, Amen!
Amen to purple sunsets, starry skies
  and morning coffee
Amen to open hands and open hearts
to signs of love
  like bread and wine
to water ever-running
and grass that's ever-green.
Amen to oil-touched foreheads
and bought-back people,
redeemed and healed and freed.
Amen to you! Amen to me!
And to the beauty of our names,
Amen, my Lord, Amen!

Then autumn came
and I was drunk with mystery all day long
Amen, Amen, Amen, I said
Amen to autumn
to mystery trees
and falling leaves
and color everywhere.

But winter told a different story. It laid on my life a message I wasn't prepared for and all my Amens stayed hiding in my heart. "Macrina," the Lord said one day, "I haven't heard an Amen for a long, long time."

"No more Amens from me, Lord," I answered. "I can't say Amen to dead and crumbling leaves, to blood poured out, and broken, ugly things. It's obvious I've made a mistake, a wrong choice. I'm taking my baptism back."

"Macrina," the Lord said again, "you didn't choose me. I chose you. And I'm not taking your baptism back."

At that moment my frightened, wintered heart remembered Jeremiah, and I bowed my head and prayed, "Jeremiah, I identify with you in your lament to the Lord. I, too, feel duped! (Jeremiah 20:7–9) Somehow He's got the best of me and I can't get away. I'm standing here with my baptism in my hands wondering what to do with it. Someone gave it to me: my parents, grandparents, the Church, my community, my God. I struggle with faithfulness. Sometimes I want to throw it all away. After all, it's just an invitation! It's too demanding! Too loving! I don't know what to do with such demand or such love. But it's too late. I've already accepted. I walked around a long time with that invitation in my heart before I said my *Amen.* But then one day I confirmed that invitation. I said *yes* to everything that God and the Church and all those faith-filled people who love me were asking of me. So you can see clearly that I've been duped! I stand here not only with my baptism in my hands, but confirmed and fed and healed as well. God has hold of me and I can't get away. I feel forever compelled to carry within me, and live out of me, these signs of God's love. Yes, Jeremiah! We must be twins. There's a fire burning in my heart too. And it's stronger than the fear." So once again I find myself proclaiming:

> Amen, my Lord, Amen!
> Amen to burning fires
>   in frightened hearts
> To brokenness and waiting
> To people still in process
> Unfinishedness and wounds.

Amen to life dug out of death
To questions yet unanswered
To winter nights and winter days
To emptiness and loss.

Amen to fragile, crumbling leaves
To crosses and to dying
To broken hearts and broken promises
Amen to shattered dreams!

Amen, my Lord, Amen!

Birth Pains

> From the beginning till now the entire creation, as
> we know, has been groaning in one great act of giv-
> ing birth; and not only creation, but all of us who
> possess the first fruits of the spirit, we too groan in-
> wardly as we wait for our bodies to be set free.
>
> *(Romans 8:22–23, JB)*

Ever since the day I was born I have been trying out loud to get hold of the mystery I find shaping my life. I have been trying to take the step that will lead me to myself. We all seem to carry within us a burning desire to be more than we are. My own explanation of this desire is that it is a call from God to grow. I take all this longing and look at it. I promise to give it every opportunity to mature. There is crisis upon crisis as I stumble toward myself. It is mystery! It is wonder! It is pain! I am settling for nothing less than heaven these days, but I am discovering that part of heaven is *loving getting there.*

It is scary to do your own breathing after the umbilical cord is cut. In an unconscious effort to remain unborn it is easy to choose new umbilical cords. They make it possible for you to blame your unbirth on others, so the walk away from yourself seems less sinful. All my life I've been being born and reborn, and the loveliest part and the bitterest part is trying to find a way to tell you about it.

I am a prisoner of life
My mother never believed in abortion
and I never believed in birth
I have stayed in the womb
I'm uncomfortable with Unbirth
but afraid of facing life
I lie to folks by breathing.

I was born one morning while I wasn't looking
I was built without a chance to look at the blueprints
I was tamed without giving my permission
but in far corners of my heart was hidden wildness
so I wrote this song for everything that was allowed
to stay wild:

Wild night sounds
somewhere in the darkness
I hear you
screaming as though there is some Egypt
you need to be delivered from.

To be wild!
To have nature's red hot blood
dashing madly through your veins
To be intoxicated
with the reality
that
no one has tried to
change
improve
or remake you!

I scream too
but I am less noisy
it is all within
  the price of being tame.

Silently I eat up the darkness
I stand
changed
improved
remade.
And pray
to be delivered
from my Egypt.

An Autumn Healing

Death, where is your victory? Death, where is your
sting? The sting of death is sin, and the power of sin
comes from the law. Thank God, then, for giving us
the victory through Jesus Christ our Lord.
    . . . keep firm and immovable, always abounding
in energy for the Lord's work, being sure that in the
Lord none of your labors is wasted.

(1 Corinthians 15:54–58)

Sometimes the autumn we long for takes place in the depth
of our hearts, instead of in our fields and meadows. The
seasons of our hearts have a way of changing our colors just
like the seasons that pass over our fields.

Such a season visited me one autumn and colored me
with life-giving death. It was the color of emptiness, and I'll
always remember how it felt. I have celebrated that color
over and over again, each time with a new understanding. I
praise God for the miracle of emptiness.

There has been no outside seasonal autumn
for me this year
no colored leaves
no falling leaves
no wind-flying, caught-up, dancing leaves
no dreams of sun-reflected colors
climbing though my window
reminding me of trees left bare
and autumn poems everywhere.

But deep inside where I like to hide
autumn walked today
like a guest awaited autumn came
and did the things that autumn always does.
It left no gold that I can see
for I am bare
and almost empty
and autumn poems I can't find.

But I wouldn't trade this autumn
for a thousand of my favorite kind.

Fire on the Earth

I have come to bring fire to the earth, and how I
wish it were blazing already! There is a baptism I
must still receive, and what constraint I am under
until it is completed.   *(Luke 12: 49–50)*

One of the powerful symbols of our Christian heritage is
fire. The Spirit of Jesus came upon the disciples in tongues
of fire. Fire burns and purifies. It destroys. It warms, and it
transforms. This transforming fire that Jesus wants to cast
upon the earth cannot be received without pain. Whatever
God's fire touches will be changed.

I long for the fire of God as much as I dread it. Who can bear such transformation? Who can be satisfied with trivia after being burned with this baptism of fire?

> I have come to light a fire
> on the earth
> Oh how I wish
> the flames
> were already leaping.
>
> Yes, there is a Baptism
> awaiting me
> How distressed I feel
> until it is accomplished.
>
> After a statement like that
> from a Person like that
> I still allow the fire of my life
> to be a simple glimmer
> instead of a flame.
>
> That Baptism he struggled with . . .
> I, too, walk around it
> instead of *into it*
> into the flame
> where death
> waits for me,
> only, to show me
> the face of life.
>
> Jesus wrestled with the fire
> but he didn't walk around the flames
> He plunged into the fire
>   into the flames
>   into the death
> When he came out
> it was Resurrection
> and his anguish turned to joy.

I am called to the same vocation
the same bath of fire waits for me,
the same God calls out to me:
    I placed you here
    to light a fire on the earth
    Oh how I wish the flames
    were already leaping
    But you have a baptism
    to receive
    and like me
    you'll be restless
    until it's over.

A Lenten Meditation

We are in difficulties on all sides, but never cornered;
we see no answer to our problems, but never despair; we have been persecuted, but never deserted;
knocked down, but never killed; always, wherever
we may be, we carry with us in our body the death
of Jesus, so that the life of Jesus, too, may always be
seen in our body.   *(2 Corinthians 4:8–10)*

The acting out of love to the extent of dying on a cross is
a mystery I have never been fully able to grasp. My limited
ability to love stands embarrassed at such extravagance. My
daily attempt to carry Jesus' dying around in my body also
falls short of my dreams. I carry my crosses carefully, trying
to make sure they don't take too much out of me.

    I always leave a little pink
    around the edges of my crosses
    I cannot bear unbeauty.

I honestly don't know how Jesus did it!
I can hardly accept *why* he did it.
The *why he did it* always makes me feel guilty
about the pink around the edges.
During Lent, at least, I'd like to let the pink go.
I'd like to be content for forty days
with a cross that isn't pretty.
But I am so young in my faith
and the vessel I carry this dying around in
is so fragile.
It is hard not to cheat a little
and search for soft, easy, pretty crosses.

O God of Lent, remember me!
Help me take the fragile vessel that I am
and fill it with your dying.
Oh, for one short season at least
let me give up my pink-shadowed crosses,
my jewel-filled crosses,
my plastic crosses.
Take all the clutter
that I try to decorate my crosses with,
all the ways I try to camouflage your death and dying
because my faith hasn't grown enough
to look at death as it really is:
an emptiness that brings me face to face with life.

And yet, within my fragile, questioning heart
I know that if I would ever dare
get close enough to dying, to death
it would fall over into life.

O God of Lent, this time you are too powerful
Your love has opened up my eyes and
the mystery is for telling.
It is my own pink-edged crosses
that have broken my heart
But your cross has saved me!

The Journey to Jerusalem

From then onward Jesus began to make it clear to
his disciples that he was destined to go to Jerusalem
and suffer grievously at the hands of the elders and
chief priests and scribes and to be put to death and
to be raised up on the third day. Then taking him
aside, Peter started to rebuke him. "Heaven preserve
you, Lord," he said, "this must not happen to you."
But he turned and said to Peter, "Get behind me,
Satan! You are an obstacle in my path, because you
are thinking not as God thinks but as human beings
do."   *(Matthew 16:21–23)*

Jesus, I don't want to be an obstacle on your path but I don't
like the sound of this journey. I hear the tone of death in all
your words these days. I can read between the lines of this
journey to Jerusalem. I fear this is not Good News. There is
a part of me that longs to go with you on this journey. But
another, more cautious part of me wants to turn aside from
anything that hints of death. I stand with Peter all the way.
I do not think the thoughts of God. My thoughts are painfully my own.

> From the cross
> the arms of Jesus stretch out
>   like wings
>   wide, all-embracing.
> So inclusive are these arms of God
>   even I am drawn in
> I, who chose not to go to Jerusalem.

I hear those words again,
    echoing in my soul
"Behold we are going up to Jerusalem!"

My eyes rest on the wood of the cross
So this is where that journey led you!
I suspected as much
that's why I didn't go.

My tightly clenched fists of fear
open just a bit
My mediocre heart
kneels down.
I lay my head into my hands
I weep softly, but not desperately
Love, like this, always makes me nervous.

The face under my mediocrity
peers out at the cross
and I ache because I didn't go.

The face under my mediocrity
peers out at the cross
and I ache
because the perfect love
that casts out fear
is not at home in me.

And yet, those arms of God
    those wings of love
keep on encircling me.
I feel incredibly taken in,
    accepted, loved.

May this wood of the cross
be my tree of life
leading me to all the Jerusalems
I still must journey.

It Is Time to Fold Your Tent

I am sure it is my duty, as long as I am in this tent,
to keep stirring you up with reminders, since I know
the time for me to lay aside this tent is coming
soon, as our Lord Jesus Christ made clear to me.
And I shall take great care that after my own departure you will still have a means to recall these things
to mind.   *(2 Peter 1:13–15)*

All of us earth-people will someday be asked to fold up our
tents and come home. Death and life stand near each other.
It is difficult at times to see where one begins and the other
ends. This meditation was written for someone who was
asked by the Lord to fold up the tent.

I am sure that in your lifetime you have known and
loved many tent-folders. This poem is dedicated, with love,
to all the tent-folders who have ever walked this earth and
to the tent-folder who is waiting in you.

> Once again death's mystery
> holds us in its arms
> and we are memoried
> with a thousand things
> you were and are, and now
> always will be.
>
> We celebrate this journey with a quiet shyness
> always a little uncomfortable
> with a mystery so deep.
> But with hearts full of life
> we hold out our hands

to receive the mystery of death
the gift of death
and sometimes we weep.

Eyes that see all the way in now
proclaim to us the new truth,
When you stand close enough to death
it isn't death anymore.
Its new name is *life,*
yet those of us with earth-eyes
still call it death.

There is really no death
for those caught up in God,
only a moment of passing over
a moment of folding up your tent
a hard, painful, giving-up moment
It is always painful to let go.

We praise a man (woman)
who had the vision to let go.
We praise a God
who had the love to ask him (her)
to let go.

O God of life
it is in our moments
of not letting go
that we truly experience death
and all the while
It is life that you have planned for us!

O God of life
dip us into the mystery of letting go
of folding up our tents
so we, your earthen vessels,
can bear the beauty of the breaking
and hold the fullness
of the life.

Do earth-people always call things
    by the wrong name?
Is it death we celebrate?
Or is it life?
Or is it letting go?

I warn you
when God gives you the grace to let go
be prepared
for a radical transformation!

Broken and Crushed

For the tradition I received from the Lord and also handed on to you is that on the night he was betrayed, the Lord Jesus took some bread, and after he had given thanks, he broke it, and he said, "This is my body, which is for you; do this in remembrance of me." And in the same way, with the cup after supper, saying, "This cup is the new covenant in my blood. Whenever you eat this bread, then, and drink this cup, you are proclaiming the Lord's death until he comes. . . ." *(1 Corinthians 11:23–27)*

Anyone who is familiar with wheat and grapes knows that the story of bread and wine is indeed a story of life and death. How wise of Jesus to use such *already sacred* signs to continue his presence among us.

We have been asked to break the bread and share the cup in His name. Each time we do this we proclaim His death and rising until he comes again.

Are not our lives a little like the wheat and grapes? Doesn't a similar kind of religious experience take place in us: the dying and rising, being broken and crushed, shared together, poured out for one another? Surely, as in that broken bread and that shared cup, it is the same Christ we are trying to recognize in the brokenness of our lives. The story of our Eucharist is, indeed, a mystery we have hardly begun to tap.

Bread too
like us
has its birth
in violence.

The seed that fell
into the ground,
died, and came forth as wheat
is now ground into new form
and flour is sifted
and changed into loaves
for rising.

We break this bread
with reverence
and give it to each other
for eating
just as another person
once broke those loaves
with us
and asked us not to forget.
We haven't!

If there is any command
we have been
religiously obedient to
it is this command of
not forgetting.
Do this in my memory!
Do it again and again!
Jesus, we have . . .
We have broken bread

with tears in our eyes
and we've broken it
when our hearts felt nothing,
but we have broken it
just as you asked us to do.
We are still trying
to understand
what it means.
But we haven't forgotten.

And the wine?
It too is born out of pain.
After days of ripening,
the grapes are crushed
and squeezed
into unfamiliar form
waiting in barrels and vats
and finally, bottles
to be accepted
loved
believed in.

And this wine also
we drink carefully
with more reverence
than usual.
It is in honor of
that same person
the One who asked us
not to forget.

And we haven't!
O God, if there's anything
we've been faithful to,
it's this
not forgetting request.

In big churches
in small crowds
   with friends
   with strangers
we meet
we break the bread
we share the cup.
And something happens
not only to the bread
and wine
but to us!

It is especially
to remind each other
not to forget
that we meet.
It is especially
to celebrate the life
that comes
out of so much death.

Bread, born out of
brokenness!
Wine, born out of
being crushed!

We are still
trying to understand
what it really means.
We are still trying
to recognize you, Lord
in the breaking and
the sharing
But we haven't forgotten!

The Prayer of a Pilgrim

O Lord of the absurd
why did you birth me into being
with not enough answers
to fill my questioning heart?

I am a pilgrim, Lord.
I'm looking for a home.
I'm death in search of life.
I'm life searching for death.

O Lord of the absurd
empty me of the meaninglessness
that stands between
death and life.
Empty me of all this unbirth.

O Lord of the absurd
teach me how to die
so I can truly live.

The Prayer of One Who Feels Lost

Jesus
My shepherd God,
If you're a shepherd

surely you should know
that leaving ninety-nine
to look for one
is kind of crazy . . .

Is that your message, Lord?
Is your love for me a little bit crazy?
Is that what you're trying to tell me?

I just want you to know, Lord
that every time I feel lost
I remember your story
of the lost sheep.

You can leave ninety-nine
to look for me
any day
even if it is a little crazy.

Prayer to a Winter God

Winter God
God of hidden face
I have been so angry
at your coldness.

I want to welcome you home
But you won't come.
We used to be friends.
That was when you came to me
in just the *right amounts*.
But now, you are too much for me.
It will take a warmer heart than mine
to hear a snow-covered gospel.

But oh, God of thawing moments,
when I allow you
to melt my frozen life

I reconsider.
My vision returns
and I know that if I am your friend
only when you come in the *right amounts*
then I am no friend at all.

Winter God
God of hidden face
you are not always spring
but your unconditional love
has touched my thawing heart
and made it warm again.

I am not always present to you
in the *right amounts* either.
Yet never have I returned
to you,
and found you
not there.

O God of unconditional love
it is an iced-in message
you are asking me to listen for
You are not always spring.

The Prayer of One Ready for Birth

O God who creates *something*
    out of nothing
Compassionate shaper of clay
Tiller of the soil
Midwife God
I am ready to be born.

I'm giving up the darkness
    of the womb.
I'm waiting for the life
    that you alone can give.

A little light
   slipped through a crack
   last night
and covered up my fears.

A promise
   leaned against my heart
   last night
and told me it was mine.

And you were in that promise, Lord
And you were in the light.
It's enough to give me hope again.
I'm giving up the night.

A Prayer for a New Beginning

O God of young faith and new beginnings
I remember the church of my childhood
where you first stepped into my life
and fed me with your life.

Your life is a treasure
I have never stopped seeking.
It is a treasure
I have never stopped finding.

I remember the deep,
ever-growing faith of my parents
who not only taught me to walk
but taught me to walk in your paths.

But now, in the middle of my years
I need you O God of young faith
and new beginnings
For the path my parents pointed out to me
seems to be a path

that leads to a cross.
and I hunger for a sign
  a rainbow
  a sprouting seed
  a meal shared with love
  a warm embrace
to assure me
that
it really is the best path.

O God of young faith
and tired faith
Breathe into my life
a new beginning.

Prayer from the Cross of My Addictions

Jesus, for so long I have carried the cross of my
addictions. I have been nailed to things that
keep me from surrendering my life totally to
you. These things that I am so attached to are
the iron bars that keep me imprisoned in the
narrow space of my own will. It is a lonely space
and far from freedom. Yet grace keeps a soft hand
on my heart, squeezing it on occasion until I am
brimming over with desire for a Savior.

Jesus, you are that Savior. You are the One who
will anoint me with the holy oil of detachment.
You are the One bringing good news to my heart.
You glance at my heart with all its broken promises
and your glance is like soothing ointment for all
the nail marks in my life.

Jesus, you are the only One who can free what is
captive in me. You lead me out of my self-made
prison and bring to me the good news of a year of

jubilee. May this be that happy promised year.
May this be the year when I let you all the way
into my life. May this be the year when everything
that is ruined, lying fallow, and unrooted in my life
be raised up, renewed, and discovered. May this be the
year when I give my energy to my heart's desire.
Dress me again in my baptismal robes for the seed is
finally taking root. I am being transformed into
another Christ. All praise to you Jesus, Savior and
prophet, sent to me from Yahweh to bind up my wounds.

So be it. Amen, my God, Amen.

A Prayer of Union with One Who Has Died

O Magnetic God. You are the Great Caller. You beckon us
to yourself. You own us. We adore you and we bless you.

Age after age you have drawn your people to yourself.
Age after age you have ushered your children into the
mystery of death and life. Sometimes the passing-over
has been quiet and full of mystery. Sometimes it has
been violent and full of blood. We who are left behind
wonder. We wonder about those you have drawn to yourself.
We wonder about ourselves in relation to those we have
loved who have died.

What we would like to see as a gentle ushering into new
life seems, at times, more like wrenching away, a tearing
from our embrace. And so, at times we are left with great
sorrow, a confusion. Sometimes we are left with a
gnawing guilt—the ache of remembering how much more
we could have been for those we loved.

O God of Unconditional Love, give us the courage and the
vision to move through the mystery of daily life with an
immense love for those who journey with us. Then we will

never need to nurse a heart full of guilt when one is
taken from us.

Loving God, you are the Great Binder. You cement our lives
together right in the middle of the Great Separation.
Continue, O Life-Giving One, to knit our lives into one
great tapestry so that we can already begin to find our
place in the Communion of Saints.

Teach us the art of passing-over graciously into this new
life. Help us to cherish our daily dyings in this School
of Life so that they may serve as preparation for our
final leave-taking.

O Magnetic God. You are the Great Caller. You beckon us
to yourself. You own us. You draw us. We adore you and
we bless you. Amen. Alleluia.

A Sunset Vespers Prayer

Jesus,
the God of Evening
has left a flaming sky.
Our earth is a home
for this Divine Artist.
To this Painter of Beauty
I cry . . .

A thousand colors is your face
    embracing us with waves of grace
And as the daystar now departs
    your glance of light fills all our hearts.

Your paintbrush streaks the western skies
    to heal the wound of all our lies
and weary hearts receive your care
    as all of heaven joins in prayer.

The evening eye shines down on earth
  a prayer for our continued birth
We lift our hearts in tender praise
  and give you thanks for all our days.

Creator God, our hearts transform
Jesus our Lord, calm every storm
And Spirit made of heavenly rays
with wings of fire sweep through our days.

The SEASON *of* FAITH

This is the after-resurrection walk! "Did not our hearts burn within us as he talked to us on the road . . .?" (Luke 24:32)

It is as important as *taking off your shoes*. It is as hopeful as *standing on tiptoe*. It is the continual acting out of that call *to wash feet*. It is the confirmation of your *racing to the tomb*, only to be surprised by life. And all these take place while *walking with strangers*.

Is this the Stranger whose coming we prepared for by taking off our shoes and standing reverently on holy ground? Is this the Stranger we stood on tiptoe for, with anxious, waiting hearts? Is this the Stranger who healed our brokenness, the One who washed our feet and carried a cross? Is this the Stranger we raced to the tomb to find? And do we race around like that to find each other?

Who is a stranger except someone whose heart we haven't met? And until you've met a heart, it can hardly bless you, can it?

The truth is that we've been blessed beyond telling by a Stranger who walked into our lives and showed us his heart, wept our tears, lived our life, and died our death.

It sounds simple and poetic except that we've been asked to do the same; for this is the Stranger who, according to Paul, left within our hearts the same power he carried in his own (Romans 8:10–11).

Trusting the stranger means we take off our shoes to prepare for the coming of each new person who walks into our lives. It means that we stand on tiptoe to wait for the coming of each person into the fullness of life. It means that we are willing to wash the feet of all these strangers and to let them wash ours. It means that we race to the tomb with them to celebrate the tomb's emptiness, which is life. Finally, it is a promise to walk with them on that journey of all journeys, *the journey within*.

Fear Makes Us Strangers

Then all the disciples deserted him and ran away.

(Matthew 26:56)

As I reflect on my own moments of abandoning people I love, I become aware of the truth that it is usually fear that drives me away.

It is fear that makes us strangers. It is fear that keeps us from entering each other's lives and celebrating who we are with one another. The only weapon strong enough to destroy fear is love. Love is often shared around a table. Perhaps this is why the Hebrew people felt so strongly about eating together. It was believed that once you ate at the same table you could no longer betray one another.

Suddenly we were strangers at that table
We had just shared the bread
We held the cup of salvation
We shared feet freshly washed by God
Yet our hearts were aching with an absence
even though, he was still present.
Something was not right
and we knew it.
We followed him to the garden
but we were no longer *one*.

Fear was clutching at our throats
   enslaving us.
We obeyed it and gave it first place
   in our hearts.
Our fear slowly overcame our love

and so we scattered
   strangers in the night.
One of us went so far
   as to deny that we knew him.
It was fear that made us strangers
   it was fear that covered up our love.

There was the cross
   the burial
   the sealed up tomb.
It was all so confusing
We were struck dumb with sadness
Somewhere our love lay
   smothered in our fears.
Our love lay buried
   with the one we loved.

Then came the journey to Emmaus,
Two of us pouring out our heart's confusion
We were joined by a stranger
   who seemed ignorant
   of all that had happened.
He listened intently
   as we poured out our story
   then gave it back to us,
   piece by piece
   explaining every fear and pain.
We were awestruck and amazed
We pressed him to stay with us
   to share our evening meal.
We weren't ready to let this stranger go.

And then, the unbelievable happened
   as startling as the moment
   when he washed our feet.
He took the bread and blessed it
He broke it and handed it to us.

We recognized him then
   a stranger no longer
   but he vanished from our sight.
That was the moment of our understanding
It was clear to us then
   why our fear started crumbling
   and why our love was returning.
Almost anything can happen at a table
Anything can happen when you share a meal.

Listening to this amazing story
I nodded in agreement
Yes, I know,
It happens at tables the world over
We sit down as strangers
   strangers in our own household.
Yet when we eat together
   the possibility remains
Some day we will leave as friends
We will drop our masks of fear
   and recognize each other
   for the first time.
How can we hand bread to one another
   and remain the same?

We've all been to our crosses
We've had our burials
We've been to the empty tomb.
Always, it is our fear that scatters us
   turning us into strangers.
Some day we will understand
   that the stranger sitting next to us
   could be our *salvation*.

Meanwhile we keep clutching our fear
   to our breasts like a cherished child.
Smothered beneath all that fear
   love waits.

Some day when our hands reach for the bread
  our hearts will touch.
And then we will know our foolishness
We will recognize each other at last
Our fears will flee away
We will be scattered strangers no longer.

Anything can happen
when you share a meal!

The Road of Trust

When they drew near to the village to which they
were going, he made as if to go on; but they pressed
him to stay with them. Now while he was with
them at table, he took the bread and said the blessing; then he broke it and handed it to them. And
their eyes were opened and they recognized him; but
he vanished from their sight. Then they said to each
other, "Did not our hearts burn within us as he
talked to us on the road and explained the scriptures
to us?"   *(Luke 24: 28–32)*

Strangers do not always have to be recognized for us to
receive their blessings. But they do need to be trusted.

The three strangers who came to Abraham's tent (Genesis 18:1–10) came bearing the good news that Sarah was to
have a child. But was it not because the stranger in them was
accepted and trusted that they were able to be a blessing in
the lives of Sarah and Abraham?

The disciples did not recognize the Stranger on the road
to Emmaus as Jesus until He broke the bread and vanished
from their sight. However, their trusting the Stranger that
he was must have begun way back on the road when he first

started to explain the scriptures to them, and they invited him to stay with them.

The Stranger you long to recognize as Christ might have to be trusted in some other form before this deeper recognition can take place.

> The road to Emmaus is not a road of the past.
> It is an everyday road
> Someone is still walking along beside us
>   explaining the scriptures to us
>   breaking bread with us.
>   and then vanishing from our sight.
>
> And we are still rather slow
>   about recognizing what's happening
>   in the breaking of the bread,
>   and that's because
>   we are slow about trusting.
>
> It takes so long to be a Church.
> We seem unable
>   to trust the struggle as divine
>   and even in the struggle
>   to cry out:
>   *It is the Lord!*
>
> We long to recognize Christ
>   before we trust
>   the stranger he sends down our road,
> And so
>   often
>   we miss the blessing.
>
> It is not that
>   we're on the wrong road.

It is rather
    that we fail
    to trust
    and recognize
    strangers.

The road
    we walk each day
    is
    the road to Emmaus.

On Giving Drinks Out of Season

When a Samaritan woman came to draw water, Jesus
said to her, "Give me a drink.". . . The Samaritan
woman said to him, "What? You are a Jew and you
ask me, a Samaritan, for a drink?" . . . Jesus replied:
"If you only knew what God is offering
and who it is saying to you:
'Give me a drink,'
you would have been the one to ask,
and he would have given you living water."

                              (*John 4:7–10*, JB)

Sometimes I get tired of walking with strangers. Sometimes
I get tired of giving drinks. One such tired moment found
me in the Kansas City airport. I was on my way to Phoenix
to give myself a drink, a workshop given by the monks of
Weston Priory.

But strangers have a way of bumping into me even
when I'm not handing out free drinks. This one was obvi-
ously very thirsty. And before I realized what was happen-
ing, I became the woman at the well (John 4:11) asking the
same kind of questions, struggling with the same living wa-

ter. Looking into the eyes of that thirsty stranger, I was able with the help of grace to notice that his well was deep and that I did, after all, have a bucket.

"Give me a drink!" he said.

> I'm tired of giving drinks
> I'm closing up my well for the winter
> I'm throwing the bucket away
> By the time I get to Phoenix
> I'll be ready for a few drinks myself.
>
> But I hadn't even gotten out of Kansas City
> when someone came up to me
> already wanting a drink.
>
> He was old
> and not used to traveling alone.
> He had just had knee surgery
> and couldn't get around very well.
> He wanted to talk.
>
> I back away in my heart.
> Everything in me said:
> "Giving drinks is not in season for me
> My well is closed for the winter
> Don't ask me for a drink
> Please don't
> I am too empty
> I am thirsty myself."
>
> But it was too late
> I had already seen his eyes
> I had already heard his voice.
> "Give me a drink," it said.

And I?

Because I couldn't avoid him
I said, "Oh, a little one maybe,
a short one
but not much.
It's the wrong place.
It's the wrong time.
It's the wrong . . ."

And then I heard it!
It was the Gospel voice all over again:
"Woman, if you but knew the gift of God
and who it is asking for a drink,
you'd ask him instead
and he'd give you living waters."

"Sir," I challenged him,
"This airport is big
and you can barely walk.
Where are you going to get those living waters?"

And the Gospel voice continued:
"If you drink the water
I have to offer,
you won't have to go to Phoenix
for drinks anymore
or to Weston Priory
or anywhere else.
In fact, you won't get thirsty again
for my drink will become
a fountain within
gushing forth eternal life for all,
and then you'll be a renewal center
for others to come
and drink from."

And I?
Well, I didn't cancel my trip to Phoenix
but I was filled
with a new kind of vision
and I knew
that
by the time I got to Phoenix
my well would be open again.

On Being a Well

"You have no bucket, sir," she answered, "and the
well is deep: how could you get this living water?
Are you a greater man than our father Jacob who
gave us this well and drank from it himself . . .?"
Jesus replied:
    "Whoever drinks this water
    will get thirsty again;
    but anyone who drinks the water that I shall give
    will never be thirsty again:
    the water that I shall give
    will turn into a spring inside him, welling up to
    eternal life."
                                    (*John 4:10–14,* JB)

The first well I ever knew was our old family well at my
childhood farm. Memories of drawing water from that well
will stay with me forever. For the most part my memories
of drawing water are joyful ones. It is true, of course, that
as a child I did not always go to the well willingly. Strange,
how our hearts change. I would give anything today for a
chance to go to that well and draw water for my family.

Although it may be too late to go to those childhood
wells and draw water for our families in reality, it is never
too late to do so in our memories. It is never too late to give

a drink to the strangers in our families, even if the drink must be given symbolically. It is never too late to become a well for our thirsty sisters and brothers in all the families of this world. Nor is it too late to receive drinks from their wells.

There are wells hidden in the hearts of all the thirsty strangers we meet along the way. Sometimes, our honest search for living water can lead us to these wells, and exchanges can be made that quench our thirst.

After the woman at the well received her drink from Jesus she became a well for others to drink from (John 4:39). In this meditation I want to challenge you to look for such wells along the way and to be such a well for others to find.

What makes this world so lovely
is that somewhere it hides a well.
Something lovely there is about a well
so deep
unpiped and real
filled
with buckets and buckets
of that life-giving drink.
A faucet will do in a hurry,
but what makes the world so lovely
is that somewhere
it hides a well!

Sometimes
people are like wells
deep and real
natural (unpiped)
life-giving
calm and cool
refreshing.

They bring out what is best in you
They are like fountains of pure joy
They make you want to sing, or maybe dance
They encourage you to laugh
even, when things get rough.
And maybe that's why
things never stay rough
once you've found a well.

Some experiences are like wells too.
People create them
They are life-giving happenings
They are redeeming experiences
They are wells,
wells of wonder
wells of hope.
When you find a well
and you will some day,
Drink deeply of the gift within.
And then maybe soon
you'll discover
that you've become
what you've received,
and then you'll be a well
for others to find.

So lift up your eyes
and look all around you:
    Over the mountains, down in the valley
    out in the ocean, over the runways
    into the cities, into the country
    sidewalks and highways
    paths in the forest
    into the hearts of a thirsty people.

Look!
And I beg you
don't ever stop looking
because what makes this world so lovely

is that *somewhere*
it hides a well,
a well that hasn't been found yet.

And if you don't find it
maybe
nobody will!

And if you don't be one
maybe
nobody will find you!

Remembered in My Heart

I always mention you in my prayers and thank God
for you, because I hear of the love and the faith
which you have for the Lord Jesus and for all the
saints. I pray that this faith will give rise to a sense
of fellowship that will show you all the good things
that we are able to do for Christ. I am so delighted,
and comforted, to know of your love; . . . how you
have put new heart into the saints.

(Philemon 4–7, JB)

Every day I take my friends to my prayer. They are remembered in my heart. During this time of remembering I
am reminded of the sacred connections that can happen during prayer. I bring a friend from Little Rock into the sacred
space within. Then I gather up someone from New York
City and walk into my heart with her. Finally all of these
wonderful people, many of them strangers to each other, are
there in the sacred space of my heart. It feels like a great
homecoming. I truly believe that these saints of God receive
energy from each other simply by being gathered together
in my heart. They may be strangers to one another but the
Christ-connection that they share makes them kinfolks.

I will be walking with strangers as long as I live. Every time I take a sister or brother to my heart to dwell, I discover that the infinite mystery of another person is so overwhelming that a part of that person will always be a stranger to me. Only when we drink the new wine together in the Kingdom will that loving stranger become completely cherished, known, and loved. On that day I will know the real meaning of friendship. Until then we will go on meeting in my heart.

Today, my friends,
I am leaving my head for a while
I am on a journey to my heart.
I am taking each of you with me
   to the oven of my heart
   to the very center
   where God lives.
I am taking you separately
   one at a time.
I take you there
   to remember you well
   like yeast remembers dough.
Remembering is a kind of loving
   a kind of baking
   and sometimes breaking.

With love, my God talks to me there
   in the oven of my heart
And shows me why it's part of heaven's plan
   that you became a part of my heart.

I remember you walking into my days
(or did I walk into yours?)
I reflect on all the ways
   you've been grace to my heart.
I remember the times
   you've been sacrament to me

a real presence for my journey, a communion
feeding my weariness new strength.

I am grateful for your presence in my life
Because of you I own a warmer heart
    a heart more breakable
    more pliable, soft and rearrangable.

When people touch me deeply
it is my heart that remembers.
And so, I remember you,
    lovingly, dearly.
I cherish you, and then . . .
I leave you there, somewhere
    in the oven of my heart.
I go back to pick up someone else
    and bring them too
    until we're all together
remembered in my heart.

I find great joy and comfort in your love
Through you my heart has been refreshed.

The Prayer of the Teacup

Never get tired of staying awake to pray for all the
saints.   *(Ephesians 6:18, JB)*

In this beautiful reminder to pray for one another the author
of Ephesians is certainly not talking about the saints in
heaven. The saints spoken of here are the saints at your
elbow, the saints in your household, and the saints you shop
with at the supermarket. They are the strangers you meet
each day.

I used to worry about how to be faithful in praying for
all these ordinary saints. While I was looking for *a way* to

pray for those who are a part of my life, *the way* found me. I call it the Prayer of the Teacup. It is a lovely way of walking with strangers.

The first fifteen minutes of each day I reserve for the saints on earth. It is one of my favorite morning rituals. I begin my day with a cup of tea or coffee. As the steam from my cup ascends to the heavens I walk with all my favorite strangers into the heart of God. There is a bit of the stranger in everyone—even friends.

This dawn prayer becomes a sacred moment of yearning. I yearn for God to bless all the peoples of the earth. And so I name my friends to God. Sometimes I do not even name them. I simply see their faces in the ascending steam. I receive the persons who come into my memory and I give them back to God. So many folks are brought together in my dawn ritual. It is as though we all become one in the heart of God: my family and friends, my community, people who have become a part of my life, those I have worked with in the past, political figures, and church leaders. Often the faces of people whose names I don't even know come to me: people at check-out counters in the stores, folks I've seen during my travels, in the airport, or on the streets. There are the faces of those I read about in the newspapers or see in the evening news. All are strangers. All are friends.

The reason I like my Prayer of the Teacup is that it is so simple. I believe that when we pray for others we often get bogged down with words. I need few words—just a name or a glance is enough. I simply look at these strangers and friends whom God loves, and I yearn for their good.

> I stand at my window and watch
> one by one the stars all leave me
> I am having tea with the dawn

the first ray of sun descending
   into my teacup
   into my heart
The steam of my tea ascending
   to the heavens
   into God's heart
The yearning in my heart streaming
   to the heavens
   into God's heart
And God, standing in the heavens
   watching the sun rise in my heart
   leans down to breathe in
   the first rays of my yearning
   and names it *morning prayer.*

(A Tree Full of Angels, p. 40)

The Discovery

May the God of our Lord Jesus Christ, the Father of
glory, give you a spirit of wisdom and perception of
what is revealed, to bring you to full knowledge of
him. May he enlighten the eyes of your mind so that
you can see what hope his call holds for you, how
rich is the glory of the heritage he offers among his
holy people, and how extraordinarily great is the
power that he has exercised for us believers; . . .

(Ephesians 1:17–19)

In small corners of our hearts are hidden bits of fear and
insecurity. And so, we do not always minister to others in
proportion to the resurrection power we possess.

   It would seem helpful then, at times, to console those
tired strangers by letting them know that it is not necessarily
their search that is inadequate. It might be, instead, our own

reluctance to come to them across the waters (Matthew 14:28).

> later
> perhaps at the end of summer
> after the corn is ripe and
> you have just put your face deep down
> into the mysterious red-green world of
> a watermelon
> if upon lifting your face
> out of that red-green world of wonder
> you suddenly know all about how
> beautiful you are
> but still feel a little undiscovered,
> please do not let me miss being rubbed
> into the richness of your life
> but come to me
>
> slowly
>   shyly
>   beautifully
>
> and hold out to me the mystery
> of yourself, because
> with the sun out and all
> it may have been
>
> my own blindness
> and smallness
> and insecurity
> —and not yours at all—
> that caused me to miss you.

Hidden Dreams

In all truth I tell you, whoever believes in me will perform the same works as I do myself, and will

perform even greater works, because I am going to
the Father. *(John 14:12)*

Some of our sisters and brothers have dreams that need
mending. If there is anything, on this journey within, that
needs investigation it is our hidden dreams.

We simply must keep each other's dreams alive. There is
a power in us that borders on the holy, and that is probably
an understatement. But what else could Jesus have been
speaking of when he told us that if we believe in him, we
will do the same miracles that he has done and even greater
ones. Jesus took his hidden dreams and gave them to us. His
dreams became a gospel. Our dreams have the same destiny.

> I am told that there are folks
> who refuse to dream
> because their dreams
> have been so seemingly shattered
> like dreams that die at birth.
> And so they hide their dreams
> in small corners of their hearts
> and pretend they aren't there.
>
> But as for me
> I am almost sure
> that in the Body of Christ
> that we call the Church
> we have the power
> to help each other's dreams come true.
> For in dark moments
> when light has hidden its face for a while
> we are the stars
> meant to shine for each other
> And we do!

More than anything else
I would like to remind you
that the dreams hidden within you
have the power
to become a gospel.

And it is as important for you to know that
as it is for the sun to shine
or the rain to fall
or a heart to beat,
because only if we believe in the gospel
that lives inside
those hidden dreams in us
can the strangers we walk with
afford to dream.

Gratitude

So he went in to stay with them. Now while he was
with them at table, he took the bread and said the
blessing; then he broke it and handed it to them.

(Luke 24:30)

Moments of gratitude for the strangers who have walked
with me fill my life constantly. There is always a return gift
waiting in my heart. It is for those who took off their shoes
to be reverent with my coming, for those who stood on
tiptoe beside me when my hope was small. It is for those
who raced to the tomb with me on the day I was certain it
held nothing but death. It is for those who celebrated my
emptiness with me and for those who broke with me the
kind of bread that fed my death new life.

the train is
somewhere in Montana
tonight
and i am on it.

softly
the god in me
wants to reach out
and give back
some of the bread
you gave me
when i was blind
and hungry
and couldn't hear.

the mountains are almost gone now
and it is getting flat
with wide-open spaces
and i feel free
like i felt
when you first handed me
this bread
and i noticed
it was different
from any bread
i had ever tasted.

because it is lasting
i am taking it back with me
to share with others
but before the dawn comes
i would like to remind you
that if things
get dry some day
as they sometimes do
and if you feel hungry
let me know
so i can send back to you
a piece of bread

for you
to break
with others . . .

A Beautiful Waste

Jesus was at Bethany in the house of Simon, . . . a
woman came to him with an alabaster jar of very
expensive ointment, and poured it on his head as he
was at table. When they saw this, the disciples said
indignantly, "Why this waste? This could have been
sold at a high price and the money given to the
poor." But Jesus noticed this and said, "Why are you
upsetting the woman? What she has done for me is
indeed a good work! You have the poor with you
always, but you will not always have me. When she
poured this ointment on my body, she did it to prepare me for burial. In truth I tell you, wherever in
all the world this gospel is proclaimed, what she has
done will be told as well, in remembrance of her."

(Matthew 26:6–13)

On some resurrection walks, my heart fills up with questions, and the gift of my life makes no sense at all. I can still
see that woman, bent over Jesus, pouring out her expensive
flask of perfume for seemingly no reason at all. What a silly
thing to do! Do not the scoffers have a legitimate complaint?
What is the point of such extravagance?

Who would think that one would become so extravagant, so wasteful, as to pour out, not only perfume, but life
itself? It is what we are all asked to do in our ministering to
the stranger in the folks we serve.

It has never made sense. It's a little bit crazy, as is all
love, to pour out your life like that. On some days, when

my hope feels small, I want to scream out with the scoffers:
"Why such waste?"

But on other days, when my eyes and heart are clear,
and I have taken off my shoes to await that stranger, I feel
immensely lavish. I feel extravagant! And with gentle conviction I proclaim: "What a beautiful waste this is!"

A jar of perfume
poured out over Jesus
and a question is born:
What is the point of such extravagance?

Why this waste?
I don't know.
I honestly don't know.
But if this shocks you so,
get ready
for you'll see more
more than costly perfume poured out.

You'll see lives poured out
    given freely
    used up
    spilled out
    wasted
for no reason at all!

Extravagance unlimited!
Lives poured out
    handed over
    lost
    thrown away
for Jesus!

What is the point of such extravagance?
Why such waste?
Beautiful questions
with no answers.

And how sad if no one
has ever asked us:
Why this extravagance?

Aren't you wasting your life on Jesus?

Song to a Silent Stranger

God whom I praise, do not be silent.

(Psalm 109:1)

During some of the seasons of my heart it seems as though
my entire life is one long Emmaus Journey. The God who
walks beside me remains so hidden and silent. A stranger
walks with me rather than a friend.

Yet slowly, as the seasons change, I move from doubt-
ing the presence of the Holy One in my life to a deep assurance that God, in Jesus, is comfortingly near. The beloved stranger sits at my table and eats of my bread. The
sharing of this bread breaks the silence. A wordless song
becomes a melody of Divine Presence.

O God whom I praise
do not be silent, I cry . . .
Yet there is no sound
no voice
no word.
Only the echo of a very old word
older than you and me
older than Jesus . . .
Yahweh, *I do not know if you are near.*

Yahweh . . .
Is that what they called you
when they were first trying to find you?

181

Were you the One riding the winds,
stirring the waters,
lifting flesh out of the earth?

O God whom I praise
do not be silent, I cry . . .

Yet the sound is so distant
the voice is so faint
the word is so old
older than you and me
older than Jesus . . .
Yahweh, *I think you are near.*

Yahweh . . .
Is that what they called you
when you were uprooting them from their lands?
Were you the One calling Abraham and Sarah
arguing with Moses
wrestling with Jacob?

O God whom I praise
do not be silent, I cry . . .

And the sound becomes a song
the voice becomes a word
the Word becomes Flesh
the flesh of Jesus
the flesh of you and me.
Yahweh, *I know you are near.*

Yahweh . . .
Is that what we call you
when your presence defies all description?
Are you the stranger who walks beside us
makes a dwelling place in us
sits at our table?

Yahweh, I know you are near.

Tourists or Pilgrims?

By Their Cameras You Shall Know Them!

Blessed those who find their strength in you,
whose hearts are set on pilgrimage.

(Psalm 84:5)

The most exasperating stranger I've had to walk with is
myself. I go through life juggling my tourist pilgrim heart.
There is a part of me that longs to be a pilgrim. I was born
a seeker. I want to travel to all the holy places of the uni-
verse, including my own poor heart. I long to stand barefoot on holy ground. I long to stack up stones in memory
of God's visitations and pour oil over them as Jacob did of
old. (Genesis 28:18–19)

But alas my tourist mentality begins to take over and the
lens of my eye is not enough. The memory of my heart is
insufficient. My albums fill up with pictures just in case my
heart forgets. My backpack turns into several suitcases as I
begin to accumulate treasures from all these holy places. I
begin to plan for new trips and regret all of the things I've
missed.

A friend tells me a story of his visit to Niagara Falls. He
was standing there in awe of that wonderful baptismal bath
when a man hurriedly walked up with his wife. The man
snapped a few pictures and then rather impatiently turned to
his wife and said, "OK Mabel, we've seen it. Let's go." Do
you think that man was a pilgrim or a tourist?

Since I am somewhat of a photographer I don't want to
belabor this point, but in sifting out the tourists from the
pilgrims I like to say, "By their cameras you shall know

them." I always remember that as I shamefacedly pass by the pilgrims with my camera. The true pilgrim is the one who has no need to capture every piece of beauty. I'm always a bit envious as I see them sitting quietly receiving the beauty instead of trying to capture it. They pray with the lens of their eyes and their hearts. They are able to gaze upon, to reverence and adore. They serve as wondrous models for those of us who find it easier to clutch, to possess, to collect.

I believe there is a hidden pilgrim in every tourist. I constantly juggle these two seekers in my life. On some days the tourist wins out. But there are many times when the pilgrim in me feels at home. Maybe I have to settle for being a tourist pilgrim.

> I stand on the edge of myself and wonder,
> Where is home?
> Oh, where is the place
>   where beauty will last?
> When will I be safe?
> And where?
> My tourist heart is wearing me out
> I am so tired of seeking
>   for treasures that tarnish.
> How much longer, Lord?
> Oh, which way is home?
> My luggage is heavy
> It is weighing me down.
> I am hungry for the *holy ground* of *home*.
>
> Then suddenly, overpowering me
> with the truth, a voice within me
> gentles me, and says:
>
> There is a power in you, a truth in you
>   that has not yet been tapped.

You are blinded
    with a blindness that is deep
    for you've not loved the *pilgrim* in you yet.

There is a road
that runs straight through your heart.
Walk on it.

To be a pilgrim means
    to be on the move, slowly
    to notice your luggage becoming lighter
    to be seeking for treasures that do not rust
    to be comfortable with your heart's questions
    to be moving toward the *holy ground* of *home*
      with empty hands and bare feet.

And yet, you cannot reach that home
until you've loved the *pilgrim* in you
One must be comfortable
with pilgrimhood
before one's feet can touch the homeland.

Do you want to go home?
There's a road that runs
straight through your heart.
Walk on it.

A Prayer to Jesus, the Stranger

Jesus,
until the day when I drink
the new wine with you
in the Kingdom of God (Mark 14:25)
you will remain
a bit of a stranger in my life.

And yet,
you are the dearest stranger
that I know.
Dear Stranger
Would you walk this road of life with me?
Would you listen if I told you all my doubts?
Would you understand if I explained
    how someone I trusted
    ran out on me?

And if we broke bread together
would the breaking of that bread
become a song in my heart?
And would I recognize you
    in the breaking
    and the song?

Dearest Stranger
It hurts to doubt so much.
Explain your words to me
the ones that stumble on my heart.

O let me know you
  in the breaking of the bread.
I'll gather up the fragments
  so as not to lose one crumb of you.

Dear Stranger
Would you walk the road of life with me?
We can walk in silence if you like
It hurts to be so full of words.

A Prayer for Calling
Home My Scattered Powers

Powers!
All around me
Beside me, Above me, Behind me.
Energy! Vibrant Life!
Lost from within me.

I am limp
from all my lost powers.

Jesus,
How did I get this way,
How did I become so emptied
  of resurrection life?
How did these Divine Powers
  become so scattered in my life?

From the ends of the earth, my Lord
I am calling home my scattered powers:
. . . Hope
. . . Faith
. . . Love
. . . Mercy and Compassion.
O Gifts of God
Come Home.

In a moment of discouragement
 you ran away
 and I let you go
But it is time
 to welcome you home.

Like a prodigal child
 you shall return
And like a grateful parent
 I'll throw a party. (Luke 15:1–24)

What was lost in me
 will come back home
What was scattered
 will be gathered together
 in the temple that I am.

From the ends of the earth
I am calling home my scattered powers
O Energies of God, come home.
Never will I send you away again.
Come home . . .

Prayer for a Questioning Heart

It seems to me Lord
that we search
much too desperately
for answers
when a good question
holds as much grace
as an answer.

Jesus
you are the Great Questioner
Keep our questions alive

that we may always be seekers
rather than settlers.

Guard us well
from the sin of settling in
with our answers
hugged to our breasts.

Make of us
  a wondering
  far-sighted
  questioning
  restless people
And give us the feet of pilgrims
on this journey unfinished.

Some Trusted Strangers:

A Scriptural Litany from the Old Testament, the New Testament, and the Now Testament

There are some strangers whom I've never met in the flesh whose stories have led me to trust the mystery within. I have come to know them and in that recognition I have been blessed again and again. These are the people who have inhabited my prayer life, who have made their home in me. Their coming into my life has enriched my pilgrim journey. They have all been a part of the gospel that has enabled me to discover Christ within the shrine of my being.

    I cannot imagine a more appropriate way to close this chapter of our unfinished journey than to walk in communion with some of the folks who have journeyed before us.

Adam and Eve
Symbols of our beginning
invited, like us,

into the process of becoming.
You understand our fragility and our glory. (Genesis 3:1–31)
Sing in us the song of creation.
Pray for us!

Abraham and Sarah
called into the darkness of the unknown
tent dwellers and stargazers
waiting and trusting (Genesis 21:1–6)
Be stars for our journeys.
Pray for us!

Isaac
Laughter of God
Child born out of barrenness
Wondrous miracle
Touch the barrenness of our lives
and teach us to laugh again.
Pray for us!

Jacob
Living on a stolen blessing
yearning for reconciliation with your brother
wrestling with an angel until dawn
Do not all of us live on stolen blessings?
Give us courage to grapple with the divine. (Genesis 32)
Pray for us!

Moses
Called forth from among the people to be a leader
begging the Lord to send someone else
fearfully receiving your moment of glory
    in taking off your shoes.
We identify with your struggle.
Give us the courage
to investigate burning bushes (Exodus 3:1–14; 4:13)
Pray for us!

Ruth and Naomi
Women of strength and devotion
attentive and loyal to each other.
We need your deep loyalty and faithfulness. (Ruth 1:15–16)
Bond us to one another as sisters and brothers.
Pray for us!

David
Desperately in need of conversion
receiving Nathan's challenge to repent.
Send the right kind of prophets
into our disordered lives.
Pray for us!

Jeremiah
Consecrated to God before birth
reluctant prophet
feeling duped and caught by the Lord. (Jeremiah 20:7)
Come to us across the desert of our reluctance.
Pray for us!

Mary of Nazareth
Mother of Jesus
woman of incredible faith
first priest of the New Testament (Luke 1:46–55)
Keep offering us to Jesus.
Pray for us!

John the Baptist
Prophet of the New Testament
prophet of passion and fire
heralding the coming of Jesus (Matthew 3:1–3)
Continue to call us to repentance.
Pray for us!

Mary
Woman of love
anointing Jesus with costly perfume (Luke 7:36–39)
drying his feet with the towel of your hair
shocking the arrogant with your extravagant love.

Lead us to pour out the fragrance of our lives.
Pray for us!

Canaanite woman
Persistent in your request to be heard
enduring the test
gathering up the crumbs of Jesus' attention
woman of faith (Mark 7:24–34)
Give us perseverance in prayer.
Pray for us!

Crippled woman of Luke's Gospel
Held in bondage for 18 years
We, too, have our demons of bondage
Enable us to stand upright with you
and glorify God. (Luke 13:10–17)
Pray for us!

Peter
Impetuous apostle
denying your relationship with Jesus (Mark 14:66–72)
yet wildly in love with this Jesus.
You understand our foolish denials
Change our apathy into burning love.
Pray for us!

Nicodemus
Aflame with a desire for rebirth
asking Jesus, *How is all this possible?*
Teach us to ask the right questions. (John 3:1–4)
Pray for us!

Samaritan woman
Talking to Jesus at the well
longing for a drink that would last forever
We, too, are thirsty for eternal life. (John 4:7–15)
Give us a drink.
Pray for us!

All you women at the tomb
Holding your oils and spices
symbols of your love for the Lord
Women in love. (Mark 16:1–6)
Grace us with feminine energy.
Pray for us!

Peter and John
Racing to the tomb
hearts pounding with expectation
believing in the empty tomb
Be with us in our race to the tomb. (John 20:3)
Pray for us!

Thomas
Apostle of honesty
openly acknowledging your unbelief
blessed, finally, through *seeing*.
Bless us in our unseeing. (John 20:24–29)
Pray for us!

Disciples of Jesus
Painfully walking the road to Emmaus
lost without Jesus
trusting the One who journeyed beside you
recognizing Jesus in the breaking of bread.
Teach us to trust the stranger who sits at our table.
Pray for us!

Paul
Apostle of the Gentiles
so convinced that this *new way* was wrong
able, with God's touch,
to change your power for evil into power for good.
Help the scales to fall from our eyes.
   (Acts of the Apostles 9:17–18)
Pray for us!

Catherine Doherty
Woman of commitment
a flame for God
preaching the gospel with your life.
We need your passion and your fire.
Smother our complacency.
Pray for us!

Mother Teresa
Gospel Woman
selfless vessel
deeply involved in beatitude living.
We need your heart of compassion.
Share with us your loving heart.
Pray for us!

Stanley Rother
Oklahoma farmer
priest, friend of the poor, martyr
icon of strength and gentleness,
shedding your blood for the poor.
Give us your hope and your laughter.
Pray for us!

Rigoberta Menchu
Woman at the foot of the cross
Guatemalan revolutionary saint
standing beside the persecuted.
Enrich us with your incredible courage.
Pray for us!

Oscar Romero
Voice for the oppressed
light in the darkness
lover of truth
twentieth century martyr.
Give us the courage to die for the truth.
Pray for us!

Jesus, Word from heaven
Making our flesh your home (John 1:14)
calling us to full gospel living (Matthew 5:1–12)
washing our feet in loving service (John 13)
promising not to leave us orphans (John 14:16–18)
Fill us with the Spirit you promised (John 16:5–16)
Pray for us!

And *you,* whoever you are
Heart so full of questions and love
trying to be a gospel person
the Body of Christ needs
the sacrament of your presence
and the power of your gospel struggle.
Send us your Christ Energy.
Pray for us!

PRAYER INDEX

REFLECTION INDEX

SCRIPTURE INDEX

OLD TESTAMENT

Genesis **3:1-31**, 190; **18:1-10**, 162; **21:1-6**, 190; **28:18-19**, 183; **32**, 190

Exodus **3:1-5**, 3; **3:1-14**, 190; **3:2**, 35; **4:13**, 190; **12:34**, 59; **17:5-7**, 83

Ruth **1:15-16**, 191

2 Samuel **12:1-7**, 15

Psalm **84:5**, 183; **109:1**, 181; **146:1**, 5

Isaiah **7:10-14**, 45; **49:16**, 70

Jeremiah **20:7**, 191; **20:7-9**, 133

Ezekiel **36:26**, 84

Hosea **3:3**, 62

NEW TESTAMENT

Matthew **2:9-10**, 51; **3:1-3**, 191; **3:3**, 45; **3:8**, 46; **3:11**, 45; **5:1-12**, 195; **5:11-12**, 96; **5:13**, 83; **5:14-15**, 83; **6:19-21**, 49; **6:25-26**, 7; **6:33**, 104; **7:7**, 111; **12:49-50**, 83; **13:33**, 56; **14:23-33**, 83; **14:27-31**, 84; **14:28**, 175; **16:21-23**, 141; **26:6-13**, 179; **26:56**, 159; **28:1-19**, 120

Mark **6:34**, 83; **6:37**, 83; **7:24-34**, 192; **9:24**, 85; **10:13-16**, 20; **10:21-22**, 14; **14:25**, 186; **14:66-72**, 192; **16:1-6**, 193; **16:2-4**, 118

Luke **1:46-55**, 191; **2:11-14**, 45; **7:36-39**, 191; **7:47**, 93; **8:43-48**, 17; **12:49-50**, 137; **13:10-17**, 192; **15:1-24**, 188; **17:15**, 82; **19:41-42**, 46; **24:28-32**, 162; **24:30**, 177; **24:32**, 158

John **1:14**, 195; **3:1-4**, 192; **4:7-10**, 164; **4:7-15**, 192; **4:10-14**, 167; **4:11**, 164; **4:28**, 33; **4:39**, 168; **8:31-32**, 130; **12:24**, 128; **13**, 195; **13:6-11**, 119; **13:12-14**, 78; **14:12**, 176; **14:16-18**, 195; **16:5-16**, 195; **16:7**, 28; **20:3**, 193; **20:3-10**, 116; **20:14-16**, 115, 117; **20:24-29**, 119, 193

201

SUBJECT INDEX